To Isobel.

with my Lo...

from. Wallace K

Psalm 23

FOOTPRINTS OF EXPERIENCE

The Memoirs of Wallace Kirkland

D1322588

Wallace J. Kirkland
5 Park Court
8A Auchingramont Road
Hamilton ML3 6JT
Tel. 01698-428013

First published 2006 by Viewfield Design
Printed by Tooth Design and Print

ISBN 0-9551764-1-7   978-0-9551764-1-8
© Wallace J Kirkland 2006

The right of Wallace J Kirkland to be identified as the author of this work has been asserted by him in accordance with the Copyright, Designs and Patents Act 1988.

This book is sold subject to the condition that it shall not, by way of trade or otherwise be re-sold, hired out or otherwise circulated without the author's prior consent.

ACKNOWLEDGEMENTS

I would like to express my grateful thanks to the many people who have contributed to the publication of this book. In particular, I am grateful to Margaret Inglis and Sandra Thompson who transcribed my recollections from tape. Thanks, too, to the editorial team at Kharis Productions Ltd: Karen Cook and May and Iain Morris for their assistance in the compilation of the memoirs that follow.

An immense pitfall that beckons any author of a book like this is the failure to be comprehensive in mentioning by name the vast number of people who contributed powerfully to many of the circumstances and events described in the pages that follow. So many of you have greatly enhanced my life's experience. If I have omitted to mention you by name, I humbly crave your forgiveness. God knows you and your contribution even better than I.

DEDICATION

To my dear wife and best friend, Nettie, who contributed so much love and meaning to my life.

Photograph by Sharp of Hamilton

"SURELY GOODNESS AND MERCY WILL FOLLOW ME ALL THE DAYS OF MY LIFE ....AND I SHALL DWELL IN THE HOUSE OF THE LORD FOR EVER." Ps23 v6

Was there ever a verse of scripture that more perfectly framed our lives in all their vulnerability and put them into the perspective of God's goodness and His eternal plan? I trust that as you read the chapters that follow you will see many illustrations of this truth in action.

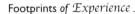

At eighty-two years of age, Wallace Kirkland is as enthusiastic about God's work as he has been for most of his life. His is a compelling story with elements that can really only be shared in a book such as this. That is why we committed ourselves to helping him communicate it and we now commend it to you.

Iain and May Morris, Kharis Productions Ltd

What a privilege and blessing to have been involved in the production of this special book and to learn of the significant ways God has worked through Wallace Kirkland. I hope and pray that readers will be inspired, encouraged and motivated by his example and that his vision for evangelism and discipleship can become yours.

Karen Cook, Kharis Productions Ltd

CONTENTS

Foreword

As I write this foreword, I'm about to step, God willing, into my eighty-second year. Every birthday, anniversary or new year inevitably finds us allowing memories of the past to mingle with thoughts about the future. Particularly as we advance in years, there may be feelings of foreboding about advancing old age and the infirmities that usually accompany it.

One day, Jesus told a crowd of fascinated listeners to "have no anxiety about anything". He made no exceptions; "anything" is comprehensive. Clearly, He did not mean that in life there would be no difficulties, no challenges, no upsets. For me, as is likely also for you, life has been awash with them. But on looking back, I can detect and trace the consoling and guiding presence of God in everything.

It has never been part of God's plan that Christians would be diverted along an easy pathway, away from the dangers and pitfalls of normal living. On the contrary, it sometimes seems that God's most faithful servants (and I certainly don't include myself in that category) find themselves facing the greatest challenges.

One day, three stalwart followers of God found themselves thrown into the heart of a massive furnace where the heat had been intensified as much as possible. Three men were hurled into that fervent heat but they were seen by their adversaries to be joined by another. God walked with them through the flames. What a picture of how God accompanies us through the circumstances of life. This book is a testimony to that experience.

What is written is more about looking back than looking forward, though one does not make complete sense without the other. My life is a journey to destination "heaven". When the last chapter of my life on earth is completed, I will have reached only the end of the beginning.

What enables me to believe that? Well, faith is a key factor, but so is my experience of God through more than eighty years of life on earth. The rest of this book is my testimony of a relationship with God in which my part has ranged from wayward child to chastened son, but in all things and in all circumstances, I can see that He has walked with me all of the way. How can one express the joy, the confidence, the gratitude for such a conclusion? As is

often the case in these circumstances, we borrow the words of another more eloquent writer: Surely goodness and mercy **have** followed me all the days of my life... and I will dwell in the house of the Lord forever.

Wallace J Kirkland, February 2006

ONE: *In the Beginning*

The Kirkland Family

Archie and Mary Kirkland were married in 1915. I was the fourth child of five, the middle boy in a family of seven people, living in a room and kitchen in Glencairn Street, Motherwell. Brother Jim, the eldest of the family, was born in 1917; my sister Jean was born in 1919 and my sister Minnie in 1921. I was born in 1924. My younger brother, George, followed in 1927. While other members of my family had fairly usual names, mine is somewhat uncommon. It was derived from my mother's maiden name: Mary Wallace.

I was born at the height of the 'depression', as it was called, though I don't think my arrival had anything to do with that fact!

Glencairn Street, where we were born - and where we went to school - is still there. These days it is not uncommon for families, at some stage, to relocate many miles from their birth places but, for Wallace Kirkland, Motherwell has been the centre of his existence for more than eight decades.

My World

This neighbourhood of ours more or less defined my world as a child. Airbles Street, Glencairn Street and Mabel Street framed my stomping territory and, even as I write this, I realise that is where I am still very much involved. The Maranatha Centre in Glencairn Street is only about two hundred yards from where I was born and another two hundred yards from there, in Mabel Street, sits Ebenezer Evangelical Church (or Ebenezer Hall as it has been known for longer), which I have attended for most of my life.

Glencairn Street circa.1925   Photograph: North Lanarkshire Council Museums and Heritage Service

Many a time I wandered around the area clasping my savings bank as tightly as I could. You see, even then, I loved to sing. I was well known around the neighbourhood and could often be found entertaining the locals – sometimes even in their homes. The only hymn I knew was "The Old Rugged Cross", and to anybody who would listen, I charged a halfpenny for one verse and a penny for two verses! They say that was when I started my professional career!!

Leisure

Beyond my immediate world, there were four cinemas on Motherwell's main street: La Scala, the Cinema, the Pavilion and the Rex. A little later, the Odeon appeared, not far from the Pavilion. In Camp Street there was the famous Empire Theatre.

The uninspirationally named 'Cinema' (or the "scratcher" as it was called) was nearest to our house and I used to beat a path there on Saturday afternoons. Entry was a penny or two jam jars! Seating was, you might say, not designed for comfort and consisted of long wooden benches with no backs. Maybe that explains the physical shape of some of us in later life! Although silent movies were the norm, inside it was anything but silent! Why? Because during the film, the patrons (us!) would perpetually be expected to warn the cowboy hero that there was an Indian at his back. Now can you understand why silence was obliterated?

Shopping

The form of Motherwell's main arteries, Windmillhill Street and Brandon Street, would be almost unrecognisable today. With the exception of the Co-operative, all the businesses were privately owned. There was Henderson's the fruit shop, Danezi's fish and chip shop (scrumptious the food was) and, still on the subject of calories, there was Crichton's sweetie shop. However, had the authorities been able to apply today's trading standards, the owner would have been arrested! All in one wee shop, she sold sweets, cigarettes, firelighters, sticks for kindling the fire, paraffin and carbolic soap: a fusion of commodities that caused the most pungent smell imaginable!

Visitors to the main shopping area in Motherwell today would find it hard to believe that, near the site of the precinct, there was once an enormous wall, about twelve feet high, running along the right hand side of Brandon Street. This wall enclosed the railway goods yard. On the other side of the street was the large Brandon Church surrounded by fifteen or twenty shops. These included Mills Music shop, selling pianos and a variety of musical instruments. There was Gray's the stationers, not only selling all types of stationery, but also suitcases and leather goods. These shops became quite famous in the area. Nearer the cross was Woolworth's. Their trademark at that time was declared on large placards placed all over the store announcing "nothing more than six pence". It is hard to imagine that they had so many goods priced at no more than 2.5p in today's reckoning. Right at the cross was the fifty shilling tailors As you can imagine their boast was that they provided men's suits for today's equivalent of £2.50. In the twenty-first century, these prices seem incredible, but consider, too, that a man's weekly wage then amounted to two pounds ten shillings - about £2.50 in today's money.

Transport

In my boyhood, transport was vastly different to what it is today. Travel, for example, was often by tramcar. I remember the tram route ran from Newmains, Wishaw, Motherwell, Hamilton, Burnbank, Rutherglen to Rouken Glen on the outskirts of Glasgow, via the city centre. As a wee boy, I could travel from the top of our street to my granny's house in Burnbank, a journey of about 6 miles which cost only a penny! My wife, Nettie, used to recount how her father would take the family (five girls and one boy) to Rouken Glen for a day out. (But only on special occasions!)

Brandon Street circa.1925

Photograph: North Lanarkshire Council Museums and Heritage Service

When not using tramcars, horse and cart was our common mode of transport. It was used for everything from carrying coal and briquettes to milk and fruit. On one occasion as a wee boy, I had to pay a visit to hospital. The highlight was being brought home in a *horse drawn carriage*! Seems incredible now.

But, of course, there was motor transport, too. One of my earliest memories is getting a 'hurl' on Frank Riddell's van. This sweetie wholesaler from Hamilton was the very first person I knew who had a motor van. He made two calls in Airbles Street, one of which was at the bottom. I used to wait for him there and be taken to Mearn Crichton's shop near the top of the street. Believe me, this was one of the highlights of my week and a very thrilling modern contrast from the more accustomed horse and cart.

Working Life

Although Motherwell is synonymous with steel making, in my childhood, the town provided other forms of work. Just off Airbles Street is Factory Road, so named because it was where the silk factory (Anderson and Robertson) was located. They employed over two hundred and fifty women working two shifts (6 am until 2 pm and 2 pm until 10 pm). The material they provided was used for parachutes during the war and, for that reason, women working in that factory were exempt from national service. The materials and the chemicals used in production were highly flammable.

Sadly, a factory that had opened on the site in 1890 was burned to the ground in 1965.

One of the recurring dominant themes in today's news bulletins is our struggle with global warming and the consequent disruption of life on planet earth. As I recall it, Motherwell's industrial base has probably made a contribution to global warming out of proportion to the actual size of the town. Even as a four year old, I well remember Motherwell shrouded in fog – or smog as it might be called today. During the winter, the fog was really bad and severely affected people who had respiratory problems. At its worst, it was known as a "pea souper". In truly Dickensian style, you could not see a yard in front of you. But there is always a silver lining: on very foggy days, you were sent home early from school .

The fog was caused in the main by the smoke from the large number of steel works in the area. Nowadays of course, with the removal of all the heavy industry, we have a cleaner environment, but the people of Motherwell and district have had to show great character in withstanding the job losses and economic blows which accompanied the winding down of our famous steel works.

Looking back on my earliest days, it seems that we were poor. But we were not poor. There were people who were a lot worse off than us. Yes, from time to time, we did borrow a cup of sugar from a neighbour and everyone was into getting "tick" from their local shop, but there was a great honesty among the people. Even with people who were given credit (there were very few of them) it was rare for them not to 'square up' at the end of each week.

Today we are well used to the benefits of social services and various forms of income support, but even in the early part of the twentieth century, poor people had access to some social benefits. People with such needs were known to be "on the parish". Unfortunately the lowly status of these families was very obvious. Boys, for example, were given special boots that were very strong. We called them "tackety boots", and those who wore them marked themselves out as being "on the parish".

During the long summer months, a significant number of children went bare foot. There were no public parks in our area so the street was where you played football, made "slides" in the winter or played with your "bogie". A "bogie" consisted of two sets of pram wheels, a plank of wood about three feet by one foot and a rope attached to the front wheels to guide it. For slides you needed a "brae" (a hill) and Mabel Street was an excellent example. In winter, when one of your pals sneaked a pail of water from the house, this was poured onto the road and quickly froze over giving you a slide. This was great fun!

A Town of Churches

If Motherwell's urban landscape was once defined by its heavy industry, its amazing concentration of churches has also given the town its unique character and symbolises the deep spiritual history of the area.

Scotland must be among the most privileged countries in the world in terms of the opportunity to hear the Christian gospel declared. Every city, town and village has easy access to places of worship. There can be no better example than the town of Motherwell.

My recollection of those early days is that the church played a greater part in the lives of people then than it does today. As I have grown older, it has been a great sadness to see so many of those great vibrant places of worship closing down. Brandon Church was demolished to make way for the development of the shopping centre. The congregation there joined with Cairns Church, now Crosshill Parish Church. Clason Church closed. It was there that a lot of my friends attended and that was where I was a member the Life Boys (number eight company). Jimmy Brown was the leader and he became a very good friend all through my life. An excellent organist and choir conductor, he became my first choice choir leader for many of the evangelistic missions during the 70s and 80s. At the church's closure, members either joined with Crosshill or South Dalziel. The Marshall Church, near the cross in Motherwell, later became the headquarters of Gospel Literature Outreach (GLO Centre) for Europe and beyond. St Andrew's Church in Muir Street closed and joined Dalziel Parish which is now Dalziel/St Andrew's Parish Church. Thankfully, that building was taken over by the Calvary Christian Fellowship under the leadership of David Simpson and has a growing, thriving ministry.

Other important congregations in the town include St Mary's Parish Church in Avon Street where I was a member of the Boys Brigade (Number thirteen company). This church today is thriving, has a big membership and is touching many people's lives. Manse Road Church served - and still does - the North Lodge area of Motherwell.

The Hallelujah Hall in Leslie Street had a silver band and had a great testimony in the town, holding regular "open airs" at the cross on a Saturday night.

Many other places of worship from the twenties and thirties still provide a vital ministry today. Many of them are Brethren Churches (Gospel Halls) - Ebenezer, Roman Road, Shields Road.

Not far from the post office corner was the Christian Institute. This was started by the then Lanarkshire Christian Union who were responsible for conducting Gospel Tent Meetings all over Lanarkshire. This was their headquarters at that time. Among the patrons of Lanarkshire Christian Union were Sir David and Lady Colville. He was a member of the Colville dynasty, owners of the Steel Works. He was also the Member of Parliament for Motherwell for quite a number of years.

The Town Mission - nearly every major town in Lanarkshire had a Town Mission - pre-dates my earliest memories.

The Baptist Church in Windmillhill Street and the Salvation Army at the top of Camp Street were both well attended and did a great job in touching many people's lives.

What a network of God-glorifying activities that surely represented wonderful opportunities for Motherwell's population over the decades to meet their creator God and to learn to walk with Him. Those who have responsibility for the ongoing ministry in Motherwell have the benefit of an enormous tradition and a great foundation on which to extend God's kingdom within this area and beyond.

TWO : *Miracle in the Family*

At any time in history, and in any place, relationships within the family are crucially important to everything else. It is in the family home that values are established and the basis for living is laid down. Although recent decades have seen increased emphasis on feminism and the rights of young people to independence, in Britain in the 1920s and for a considerable time thereafter, 'father' was the dominant influence.

Archie Kirkland, my father, was a master mason and involved in a Monumental Sculptors business in partnership with his brother James. For around a hundred and twenty years, the firm, known as James Kirkland Ltd, was a well known business in the town. However, owing to the very difficult times experienced in the depression, my father had to take a job in Dalziel Steel Works.

My dad was Motherwell born and bred. My first memory of him was seeing him lying, under the influence of alcohol, stretched out on the kitchen floor. A fierce man when drunk, the only person who could handle him in that condition was Aunt Minnie Hill - a holy terror - who was able to put my father in his place more ably than my mother who was a more gentle person. She had to put up with an awful lot in these early days. My memories of the curse of alcoholism and drunkenness are very vivid. A good, caring, jovial husband and father when sober, drink transformed him into a man we scarcely recognised. I am sure that the economic situation of the times exacerbated my father's need for alcohol and our home was not the only one, by any means, to be adversely affected.

I cannot remember instances of physical abuse, but there was verbal abuse a-plenty and the problem existed over a year or two. I do remember one evening my elder brother Jim coming in late. Father must have belted him because he landed at the bottom of the stair! Emotionally, I used to cower from these events. How my mum was able to handle the problem with seven of us living in a room and kitchen is a tremendous credit to her. For a child, it is devastating when their parents row. Sadly, in some homes, it is an every day event. I felt very tender hearted towards my mother but I also felt helpless in the situation, often simply asking in a hapless sort of way, "Mum, will you be all right?"

One positive role I did try to play was to meet my Dad emerging from work. Friday was pay day and so there was a special temptation to spend the hard earned wages in immediate escape from the doom and gloom around. My job was, if possible, to steer father past "The Hairy Man", the local pub that proved to have such a magnetic pull on him and which was the origin of so much of our family's distress. My plan never worked. While my father imbibed in "The Hairy Man" (a horrible name for a horrible place) I had to wait outside before taking him home. He usually gave me a halfpenny, probably to keep me quiet. One day it all changed. The reason? The impact of Jesus Christ upon his life.

During his unconverted days my father would have been God-aware to some extent and might even have had some knowledge of the gospel. There was so much evangelical activity pervading the community – open airs, tract distribution, salvation army bands. You could not remain unaware and we have to ask ourselves how we respond to the ignorance of the gospel that is so prevalent around our streets today.

An example of God-awareness was the decision taken by my parents to have the whole family christened, just after my arrival in 1924. Jim was 8 years old, Jean 6, Minnie 3 and they had never been christened! The minister who performed the ceremony was the Rev Duff McDonald of South Dalziel Parish Church. It is obviously difficult for me to remember this, but as I look back, I thank God for that time. And, for sure, it was the hand of Jesus Christ in his life, and not the christening of the children, that would be required to give my father the power to change.

Evangelism, through children's work, is a time honoured and well tested means of bringing many to faith and so it proved in our family. My older brother Jim had been attending the Sunday School and Bible Class at Ebenezer Hall and he had become a Christian. This was followed by my mother through attending the women's meetings.

So it was that, through the connections of other members of his family with Ebenezer Hall, my father found himself exposed to the gospel. Whether on the first or the tenth visit, I do not know, but I am sure that he committed himself to the Lord. Whisky was changed into furniture and darkness turned to day.

In recent days I have been saddened by the number of young people who have become disillusioned/sidelined/disenchanted by what they perceive to be "the church". Some of the disillusioned are among my own young family members. However, as I look back, I realise I was no different. The age when this sense of detachment kicks in is often around fifteen to eighteen years of age. I can so empathise with how they feel and react. It would be a desperate mistake to assume that the church is beyond reproach in how it attempts to relate to young people. What a challenge to try to communicate spiritual realities and practicalities to the teenagers of today who live in a world of extreme materialism and utter confusion with morally baseless value systems. As a man of mature years, I hope I have the benefit, not only of being able to look back, but also of bringing a mature understanding of what is really important in living life. If only our young people could find the motivation and the wisdom to see the fundamental importance of living life based on Christian faith! All else places them in an utterly vulnerable situation which they attempt to control but which is massively more powerful then they are. If Christ is not the centre of gravity in their lives then something else is. That something will pull them in its own direction. I know this from personal experience and from observation.

The basis of Christian faith is a strong belief in the importance and the power of the gospel, not only to save us for eternity, but also to change our lives which have been weakened and crippled by sin. My father's conversion was just one example, but a powerful one, of how God can change lives.

I believe that a major influence in my father's conversion was the work of a genuine prayer warrior, Mrs Sinclair. She was a soul winner par excellence. Not content just to pray for people or attend church services, she was determined to do everything she could to see people won for Christ.

Hannah Sinclair and her husband sat in the second front seat in the gospel meetings in Ebenezer Hall. I believe that, because she prayed so much for people, God gave her insight and wisdom. She knew when to approach people, what to say and, through prayer, she saw things happening under God. She was a special lady and a wonderful role model whose influence still guides me in my attitude to, and practice of, prayer.

Mrs Sinclair was the means of all our family coming to faith. Brother Jim and sisters Jean and Minnie had gone to Sunday School, following the strongly held social tradition of the time. Most children, following the sweetie trail, went to more than one Sunday School. For us this included the Salvation Army, Crosshill Church and the YMCA. This organisation has been a great help to very many young people and continues to this day. We also attended the Band of Hope on a Monday night in Cairns Church, at the top of Airbles Street - now Cairns Parish Church - where hundreds of children gathered to learn Bible based choruses and then watched with awe and wonder a new invention called the 'magic lantern'. Let's not forget that there was also Ebenezer Hall, of course! We went to Sunday School there too.

Around this time my Sunday School teacher was Archie Tool who lived in North Lodge Avenue. I remember visiting his home once a week in the run up to the Sunday School soiree and having to learn the words of Isaiah 55. As I look back, I thank God for the commitment of people who, like Mr Tool, encouraged young people to memorise the scriptures. This does not seem to happen so much these days. As a result of members of my family and particularly my father coming to faith, there was a radical change in our circumstances. We were able to afford to move out of our room and kitchen in Airbles Street into a three bedroomed burgh house in what I reckoned was the best area in Motherwell – number one Cunningair Drive in the North Lodge area of the town.

Looking back, it is fascinating to see how my father's life, influenced by the Holy Spirit, changed every other aspect of living as well. Scripture tells us we are made in the image of our creator and so it is hardly surprising when more beauty and more ordered living result from lives that have been spiritually re-connected with their creator. So many of us know the theory, yet it is still a wonder that we find the practice so difficult. Thankfully, in our family, we experienced the reality of a new relationship with God and so many of its advantages.

THREE : *From School to Working Life*

It was from No. 1 Cunningair Drive that I started school, aged 5, at Glencairn Public School about half a mile from my home. Although school was never a favourite place for me, I have some lively memories of life the classroom.

Mr McGovern was the headmaster, a very jovial type of man - that was until you were sent to him for misbehaving! Say no more! In these days, I was one of about forty children in one classroom, with two people at each desk working

Glencairn Public School
The young Wallace Kirkland: back row, extreme right

side by side. I say we worked 'side by side', not 'together'. Whereas, today, children in school are encouraged to work co-operatively and to interact, these were more Dickensian days of individual work and silence. Miss Gibson, the class teacher, had her own inimitable way of ensuring isolation. "Now turn around bum to bum," she would order. She was something else! And so in enforced solitude we would scratch across our slates, and our education laboriously progressed line by line.

Later in school, I was taught by Miss Pollock She came from Carluke, I remember. There was great excitement when we discovered she was going to get married. Everyone in the class brought their individual wedding present, each person trying to impress more than the other. Even as I write this I remember her face so clearly. It is impressive how even between children and adults there can be an important chemistry that affects the total relationship and helps us feel that we know this other person in so many ways. Miss Pollock impressed me greatly and, as a result, I had the conviction that she would go on to be a good wife and mother.

It was around this time, aged 6 or 7, that I learned to swim. Swimming was soon to be a passion of mine and an important way of expressing myself, as well as being something I could do well. A near neighbour of mine was a senior baths attendant. His teaching method was uncomplicated: he pushed you in at the deep end and held out a long pole. It was truly sink or swim! His name was David Neilson and he later became the baths master at Wood Road open air pool, Cumnock, before becoming the baths master at Clydebank. He became a great friend. Meanwhile, on my mother's initiative, there were other skills to learn!

You have heard it said that "you can't make a silk purse out of a sow's ear". My mother was determined to prove that wrong. She sent me to elocution lessons, to Mrs Jean Weir, who stayed only fifty yards away from us. No doubt you are expecting me to say how I attempted to escape the elocution regime and managed to convince my tormentors that this was not for me. On the contrary, I can scarcely believe how highly I achieved and I have the examination certificates to prove that I passed with high grades, going on to the last but one exam that would have given me the coveted qualification of ALCM. Can you imagine it? Wallace Kirkland, ALCM! This would have qualified me to become a teacher - a status which incidentally both my sisters, Jean and Minnie both achieved.

The exams were held in St Andrew's Halls in Glasgow. Try to imagine Wallace standing in the middle of an enormous stage, addressing an audience that consisted exclusively of three adjudicators. As I envisage their faces, even now I think they would turn milk sour! So there you have it. Wallace Kirkland was only one step away from becoming an elocution teacher. Nevertheless, even today, I am sure that everyone who knows me can detect the cultured tones of my voice!

Meanwhile, the family was continuing to benefit spiritually – and economically - from my father's now stabilised life. If ever I am asked if I believe in miracles, this change in our family life is the first thing to spring to mind.

Father's business was doing well again and this enabled us to move to 130 Manse Road, Motherwell, a private house with more space for the seven of us.

Living next to Dalziel Estate was a big attraction for me. I became friendly with the gamekeeper, Mr Gibb and his family and I used to help him (or so I thought) with the cleaning out of the kennels. At that time, they housed three or four lovely English mastiffs. Lord Hamilton was often in residence at the "big house", and on a few occasions I was asked along with others to "beat for the shooters". As instructed, I had to move through the woods towards the guns, flushing out the many pheasants.. I loved being involved in this as it included having breakfast in the kitchen of the "big house". Jessie Gibb, the daughter of the gamekeeper, was a lovely blonde girl and a lot older than me. She had the job, in the spring of the year, of looking after the young pheasants at the hatchery on the estate. They reared many hundreds of pheasant chicks and, of course, these were a great attraction to hawks. She was able to handle a double-barrelled shotgun to great effect. I remember that time very well. Jessie later became the first female in Scotland to qualify as a motor mechanic. I don't think there are too many of them even today, the good looking ones I mean.

Also on Dalziel estate was the home farm which proved a great attraction for me. My boyhood pal at that time was Alex Thomson. His father worked on the estate and they lived in one of the farm houses. In the summer, the farmer, Jock Howison, gave me a job. I got 7/6d a week for working a whole lot of hours, but I loved this particularly when I was given the job of working with the tracer horses because most of the crops being harvested were down in the haugh just beside the River Clyde. There was a clever system for bringing the crops from the riverside up hill via a steep climb to the farm. At the start of the incline, the tracer horse was hitched to the cart. In turn, they were hitched to the other horse already positioned on flat ground at the top of the incline. Now we had a two horse-power job. For a boy of twelve this was exhilarating: leading and coaxing the tracer to give of its best. And I got paid for it!

One poignant memory of the harvest time was when at the lunch and tea break the big hamper arrived with some great food concealed inside. For me food anywhere, anytime, was always good news.

It was around this time my mother and father decided I should change schools. No doubt they had realised that I was not performing too well at Glencairn Public School and they believed that, by enrolling me at Hamilton Academy, this might bring about a change. A forlorn hope for a non-achiever like me! My new school was fee-paying and, on looking back, I appreciate that they wanted to do the best for me, but sadly, I didn't have much taste for academic work. I did, however, thoroughly enjoy my involvement in rugby and cricket. My recollections include the bruises as well as the sport.

Back in the classroom, I remember on one occasion getting only twenty-three per cent for my French. My only excuse was that the teacher was a lovely blonde French lady and I was much more taken up with her than with the language. My captivation was greatly enhanced by the fact that I sat in the front row!

And then, would you believe, we were on the move again. When I was aged fourteen, we transferred to a bigger house at 9 Orchard Street, Motherwell. One big advantage of this move was that we were now living only two hundred yards away from the local swimming baths and this was where, for the next few years, I would spend each evening, Monday to Friday, and also some Sunday afternoons (unknown to my parents).

The Lanarkshire Olympians

Photographs by Walter C Van Rooyen, Glasgow

In the late thirties and forties and even extending into the fifties, Motherwell's swimming talent was held in very high esteem throughout the United Kingdom, and rightly so. Much of it was to the credit of David Crabbe, the baths master, between 1935 and 1968. Not only was he a great coach and disciplinarian, he was also a wise counsellor, and to many, including myself, a great friend.

As I look back, I was privileged to be part of this group of swimmers but being called up to the Royal Navy, just after my eighteenth birthday, cut short my further involvement.

Mr Crabbe coached local people to great proficiency in swimming. Included were such household names as Nancy Riach – the most famous swimmer in war time Britain - Nan Rae, Cathie Gibson together with British and European champions. Nancy Riach sadly died of polio while she was taking part in the European swimming championships at Monte Carlo in France in 1947. It is estimated that ten thousand people lined the streets of Airdrie at her funeral. She was a lovely girl.

Among the men who also experienced great swimming success were the Wardrope twins (Jack and Bert), Jack Ferguson and Forbes Gentleman. Motherwell's famous swimmers participated in the Olympic Games in London (1948), in Helsinki, Finland (1952) and in Melbourne, Australia (1956) where several of the Motherwell Club members took part in water polo and swimming events. Amongst those selected were Cathie Gibson, Nan Rae, Jack and Bert Wardrobe, Jack Ferguson, Ian Johnston, David Murray, Forbes Gentleman and Jim Gibson.

I may not have shared the proficiency of the champions, but I certainly shared their enthusiasm and, although not harmful in itself, I believe swimming was a major factor in my losing interest in the meetings of the church. They held no apparent relevance to my life. I was too intent on involving myself in the things that I liked. In fact, I was glad to have the opportunity to leave home. The war being on, I volunteered for service in the Royal Navy aged seventeen.

However, on looking back, I realise what a big influence Mr Crabbe had been on my life. He had a strong Christian upbringing, but on seeing the impact and extent of the "depression", he became disillusioned and appeared to reject what he had been brought up to believe.

Sadly, it is all too typical of our limited human understanding that when life presents major obstacles and difficulties we conclude that faith in God is misplaced. When we abandon trust in Him, we are then thrown back on our own feeble intellectual resources to try to make sense of everything. I would suggest it is such a mistake to put so much faith in our own ability to reason things out. It is an act of utter simplicity and naivety to think that we can reach a point in our reasoning where we can dismiss God from the equation. There are so many things that we can never understand but instead of realising that in humility, we adopt an arrogant posture and dismiss God from our lives because what we believe He has done does not fit with how we think we would have acted if we had been making the decisions that are His to make.

We should never give up in our efforts to pray for those who have "left their first love". I remember presenting a copy of my first LP (entitled "The Happy

Heart") to Mr Crabbe, in appreciation of what he meant to me. He became quite emotional. This was unusual for him. He complimented me on the work I was doing among young people and when I told him that *his* influence on me had contributed to my great interest in those young people, it seemed to touch a chord with him. I remember visiting him in his latter years at his home in the Jerviston area of the town. He sat down at the organ and started to play some of the old gospel hymns and I sang to his accompaniment. Let us never underestimate the power of early Christian influence to return at any point in later life.

At this point, it is appropriate for me to comment on the strong Christian influence in my own young life. I had lived through a very important time of change in my family's circumstances. After my father's conversion, all of us attended Ebenezer Gospel Hall on a regular basis.

Sunday was the busiest day of the week. The Breaking of Bread service started at 11 am and lasted until 12.30pm. The Bible Class was at 1.45pm. At the age of twelve, I was old enough to qualify for the Bible Class. (The age range was twelve to eighteen years.) The leaders were Robert Anderson and Willie Brown and, looking back, I realise what a good job they made of leading the Bible Class. Along with their wives, they arranged many outings - rambles they were called - to various places within easy reach of Motherwell during the summer months. They also arranged parties during the winter. The food at these events is maybe what I remember most vividly, not unusually for me.

However, having been influenced by the teaching from God's Word, as well as having witnessed the change in my father's life (along with so many more families like ours, whose lives had been turned around), at the age of twelve, I committed my life to Jesus Christ. I can remember that event clearly after all these years. Again, Mrs Sinclair played a crucial part. As I look back, I can say without fear of contradiction that she was the greatest soul winner I have ever known. At the end of each evening service there was always a challenge made to commit your life to Jesus Christ. As the Sinclairs were moving out, and having prayed for specific people (younger and older), Mrs Sinclair would invariably just quietly speak to the person uppermost in her mind and ask if they had considered making the all-important decision to become a Christian. Such was the occasion on 12 December, 1936, when she spoke to me and simply explained what was required of me to be born into God's family through simple faith in the Lord Jesus Christ, believing that he died for my sins on Calvary and that He was buried and rose again on the third day and then went back to heaven. I had known these facts in a general way, but, that night, I accepted the need to commit my life personally to Jesus Christ and I look back on this with great joy and assurance.

Swimming and water polo were still a big part of my life at this time. Our club was Motherwell YMI (originally associated with the YMCA). We were often asked to provide swimmers for competitive events up and down the country, usually opening galas in coastal towns such as North Berwick, Prestwick and Troon. Typically, this would be in late May and, invariably, it was very cold. However, there were prizes to be won and that was a great incentive.

The open-air pool that a lot of my friends and I liked most was the one in Wood Road in Cumnock. This, as far as I know, was the only outdoor swimming pool not on the coast. The baths master was David Neilson. A number of my friends used to cycle to Cumnock from Motherwell, a distance of around thirty miles. This divided very nicely into three sectors: ten miles to Strathaven, another ten to Muirkirk and the remaining ten to Cumnock. My friend Tom Ferguson and I were the youngest of the lot and were well looked after. On a Saturday night we would go to the dancing in the Town Hall there - that's where the 'talent' was and the natives were very friendly. One memory of that time was the occasion when we were returning to the campsite beside the baths. Just across the Lugar burn was Spiers bakery and, at that time of night, it was very quiet and we used to get into the back of the bakery and nick a few of the goodies and take them back to the tent and have a nosh up.

I have since been back to Cumnock. The most recent time was to take part in an evening service at the Church of Scotland where my nephew Ross Adams and his wife Myra and their family are members. After the service, one or two of the members spoke with me. They remembered the time when the lads from Motherwell came to the Wood Row baths. We were able to share some memories and I was anxious to know how they were after all these years. When I look back on the times of travelling to Glasgow, Edinburgh, Dundee and elsewhere in order to play water polo, I realise we did it for love, not money. The expenses we received were 2/- (20p in today's money); just enough to buy a fish supper on the way home.

In 1939, I left school (one of the best days of my life!) and started work in Colville's Dalziel office. It is hard to imagine now that, at fifteen, I was still wearing short trousers! There was no difficulty getting a job at that time, particularly since so many men had gone off to war. Everyone left in Motherwell was in some way involved in the steel works. All around the town there were so many – the Clyde Alloy, Lanarkshire Steel Company, Colvilles Ltd, Dalziel and all the ancillary works like Anderson Boyes, Findlays, Motherwell Bridge. Even our glorious football team was called "The Steel Men". Because of the war all of these businesses were working to full capacity to meet the demand for steel.

Why was my first job in Colvilles? Well, dad's younger brother, Jimmy, had worked in Colvilles. He started his own steel stock holding business and was doing well and he wanted me to join him. His office was in Glasgow. He bought me books on steel making but, as a boy of fifteen, I was just not interested in it at all. So instead of going to work with him, I started as an office junior in Colvilles. I worked first in the postal department and I reckon (and many others would agree) I was the worst office boy ever. The job involved opening the mail first thing in the morning, distributing it to the various departments in the office and the rest of the works and, in this way, I got to know all the heads of departments, the melting shops 1, 2 and 3, the test house, the engineering shop, the rolling mill and the plate mill. We will draw a veil over other incidents!

Looking back, that was quite a time in my life. In recent years, I have been reminded about my behaviour, particularly with some of the women, who worked in the office, who once alleged that I locked them in the very large walk-in safe.

Each year, one of the highlights was the staff dance. It was a posh affair and, as the office junior, I was given a free ticket. The event was always held in the Hamilton Salon which, in these days, was the premier ballroom in the area. The ladies wore long evening gowns and the men sported bow ties and dinner suits. On one particularly snowy evening, I went outside, gathered some snow, and, as the ladies floated around the floor, I dropped some snow down the back of their dresses. That little prank earned me a good few serious rebukes – particularly from the men!

All of the foregoing - school, Sunday School and work - is part of the great academy of teaching, but there were many more lessons to be learned in the school of life.

FOUR : *In The Navy*

Young Wallace. Week 1 in the Navy

In 1941, aged seventeen and two years after the commencement of the war, I volunteered for the Royal Navy and was called up just after my eighteenth birthday. Had I not volunteered for the Navy, I would more than likely have been called up to the Army. I would not have been too happy with that.

On receiving the call, the first thing I had to do was to report to St Mungo's Halls in Glasgow. The day I left home was quite traumatic. My mother and my sister Jean, in particular, were very distressed as I left the house on my way to active service. My father came to the bus station to see me off. Probably to try to raise my spirits a bit, he quipped, "Don't worry too much about the war, son. When the Germans know that you've enlisted, it'll be over in a fortnight or so!"

I travelled on the number sixty-four bus from Motherwell, through Hamilton and Rutherglen, into Glasgow. I sat upstairs on the double-decker and I think I cried most of the way there. So much for this tough guy, Wallace, thinking he was a man.

When I arrived at St Mungo's Halls, we were ushered into a large room. There were about forty to forty-five people, all of them seeming so much older than me. It was announced that we had to travel to Plymouth. After our names had been called from a register, I was, for some reason, nominated to be responsible for the people on the train and to report to the Chief Petty Officer at Plymouth. That might seem as if it were an honour, but let me tell you it was no honour!

When we arrived at Glasgow Central Station, I stood with the ticket collector and started to check the names from my sheet but, as time went, on the men were rolling in drunk and it was impossible to make sense of what was happening. I opted to allow all of the guys present to get on board just hoping that everybody was, indeed, 'present and correct' for the overnight train journey down to Plymouth.

I remember arriving there and the Chief Petty Officer asking if everything was in order and, with absolutely no confidence, I replied that it was. Quite honestly, there was no way of knowing if everybody on that sheet was on that train.

We were taken from there to HMS Raleigh where I did my six week basic training in seamanship.

Plymouth is an impressive city, located on the south coast of England, but sadly, while I was there, it was bombed fairly regularly and it was a frightening time. On various visits to the city, it was awesome to see the devastation that the bombing had caused. What an initiation for me, because I was scared out of my wits. I recall on one occasion returning from being ashore and having to crawl along hedgerows, so scared I was about the proximity of the bombing. This level of fear was entirely new to me.

Before I left home, I had promised my mother that I would attend church and I endeavoured to do so. I assumed that finding a Brethren church in Plymouth would be very easy but it proved otherwise. However, I believe that the Lord was in all of this. In my earnest efforts to find a church, I enquired in a large police station as to whether they knew the whereabouts of a place of worship for Christian Brethren. At first, they appeared unable to help me. Just as I was leaving, however, a policewoman indicated that the place I was looking for might be located about a mile and a half away from the police station and pointed me in the direction. I remember walking there and arriving late, but I went in anyway. The normal meeting place had been bombed and the church members had convened in a large wooden hall.

As I opened the door, I must have made a noise, for an old woman looked round and beckoned me to come and sit beside her. I can tell you that was very, very special. The lady's name was Mrs Bellechamber. Subsequently, her family and I became firm friends and they looked after me very well. Afterwards, my mother kept in touch with Mrs Bellechamber and they exchanged gifts from time to time.

Mr & Mrs Bellechamber

Others who showed me great kindness at that time included Mr & Mrs Hill. They attended another Brethren Church in Plymouth. Strange to think that their church, one of the biggest in the West of England, was in the same street as the police station where I had made my original enquiry about the Brethren church. I was convinced, of course, that the Lord was in all of this, taking me into the home and love and affection of the Bellechamber family.

On one occasion, having gone home with them after a church service, they asked me if I had any connection with a James Kirkland, also from Scotland. Amazingly it turned out that my elder brother Jim, having been evacuated from Dunkirk during that terrible exodus from Europe, had come into Plymouth and had, indeed, been hosted by the same family. What a great encouragement it was to me at that time to feel, and to know, the tremendous benefit of loving Christian hospitality.

FIVE: *All at Sea*

Meanwhile, on completion of my training, my first posting was to Campbeltown where I volunteered to be an anti-submarine detection operator.

I attended the little Brethren church in Long Row in Campeltown. At that time, it was really quite a strong church with a good number of people in membership. Many of them were fishing people and included a Mr & Mrs Short. They lived in Long Row. They were very kind and looked after me. I was also indebted to the family who owned and operated the local bus service, West Coast Motors. On a Sunday evening Mr & Mrs Craig would invite me to their place for supper and that was a lovely experience. I always had to be back at the base before 11pm. As they stayed out in the West Bay, I had to run all the way from their home right back to the station, but it was well worth all the trouble for they were such lovely people.

Young Wallace puts to sea

The Campbeltown tour of duty was the first time I had gone to sea. As part of the course I was on, I had to do practical training on board trawlers which were specially fitted with anti-submarine detection gear. The submarines would be well out in the Irish Sea and our task was to locate them. That coincided with my first encounter with sea-sickness and I can tell you it is not an experience that anyone should relish. I remember being on the bridge and feeling that I needed to be sick. While I was making my way down, I met the duty officer who was on his way up. "Kirkland," he said, "where are you going?" At that point I opened my mouth to tell him and was sick all over him. Not a great experience – particularly for him!

When my time at Campbeltown came to an end, I was then transferred to Dunoon. The naval base was called HMS Osprey. It was located in the old co-operative home, a huge establishment and it was from here that we were posted to our various ships.

On Board HMS Guardian

My first ship was HMS Guardian and I had to join that in Belfast. I don't remember seeing anything of the city of Belfast itself as the ship was ready for sailing pretty much as soon as we had gone on board. Interestingly, the first trip was back over to Scotland to the 'tail of the bank'. It is the part of the Clyde that opens up at Greenock and Port Glasgow. There, we were to join a convoy that would move out to sea. Before departure, we were given leave to go ashore at Greenock From there, I telephoned my mother and she arranged to be at Largs on the following day. I was able to meet her there. She had gone to visit a Mr & Mrs Watson who lived there. This re-connection with the family reminded me of the emotional challenges of leaving home at a tender age in order to play a part in a war situation. Having spent an evening with my mother and the Watsons, I returned to the ship and the next day we set sail.

As we sailed gracefully out of the Clyde, we passed Largs on the port side. It was very early in the morning and the steeples of the churches in the town stood out starkly against the sky. I thought about having seen my mother the night before and, acutely conscious of how this vessel on which I was standing would take me relentlessly away from home, the tears started to flow.

Supporting the war effort in Gibraltar!

We sailed into the Irish Sea and made our way to destination Gibraltar. I don't remember too much of the voyage between 'the tail of the bank' and Gibraltar because I was sick most of the way. One of the things that kept my spirits up was that I knew Gibraltar was a place of sunshine and at least I was looking forward to that.

On arrival, it was interesting to see 'the rock'. Such an historic place! There, we were able to go ashore and swim and enjoy the beach on the far side of 'the rock'. Not a bad experience at all, but not one either that, at this point, was contributing much to the war effort. In fact, war seemed part of another world. However, we were to be rudely awakened about the reality of our situation.

On one occasion, returning to the ship, we saw smoke coming from the dockyard. We discovered that the problem was on board our ship. We concluded that it had been sabotaged and so, quickly, we had to set about doing some repairs.

If, previously, the war had seemed a distant reality, our imminent involvement was now borne in on us very strongly. Information reached us that we were now going to be part of the invasion of Sicily that would extend through Italy. Getting the ship patched up was a top priority and we left Gibraltar to join what seemed like hundreds of ships moving through the Mediterranean Sea.

I was enchanted with the colour of the water, the light, light blue. I was struck by the amazing contrast between the beauty of the environment and the reason we were there. At first, it felt like a pleasure cruise, but, once again, relaxation turned to tension as we approached the coast of Sicily where we gradually became aware that we were increasingly within bombing range of the German and Italian troops in Italy.

We reached Sicily safely and I well remember being in Messina in the north of the island. Our ship had a very specific role because, while we had gunnery instructions and various other weaponry, our main purpose was to follow on behind the Army. They would secure the land position close to the port and we would move in. More specifically, the task of our ship was to lay nets in the form of booms across the mouth of a harbour so it was as safe as possible from any intrusion by enemy submarines or even surface ships. We did this in various ports on the east coast of Italy.

However, there was evident concern that our ship had been damaged in Gibraltar and a plan was put in place for the ship to be repaired in Malta. On arrival, we sailed into Grand Harbour. What a glorious sight; such a beautiful natural harbour but what a contrast with the devastation to the whole of the island. It had been bombed and was a terrible sight to see. On going ashore, I saw little but rubble. Nevertheless, for the resistance that they had put up, the islanders certainly deserved the honour of being awarded the George Cross. Malta is known around the world as the George Cross Island.

One particularly sad memory of Valletta - the capital and the location of the Grand Harbour - was the sight of women (not just young lassies) swimming out to the ship and clambering aboard. We allowed them to do so on account of an edict from the skipper. Our 'boarders' went through the 'gash buckets' and took away anything that was remotely edible. It was sad to see those people rummaging so vigorously and taking away, in bags, our leftover food.

We were moored for a time in one of Malta's famous locations: St Paul's Bay. More recently, I have seen in brochures photographs of St Paul's Bay displaying attractive buildings and hotels, but I tell you that, on my first visit, this was a place with just one or two farm houses on the side of the hill and one or two vineyards coming down to the waterside.

We used to go ashore on one of our boats and 'steal' (that's the only word I can use) grapes from the vineyards and take them back to the ship. That was nothing to be proud of - it was just one of the things I can remember doing. Perhaps it is seared on my conscience.

During that time, life was not all heroic action and, indeed, I got an opportunity to use my swimming prowess, developed in my earlier days. We were able to play water polo and, from time to time, during the three months we were located there, I was taken around to Valletta to swim competitively against other teams from the army. And then there was rugby. Can you imagine playing rugby, not on a grass pitch, but a hard pitch? It was painful.

While we were in St Paul's Bay, there had been major developments on the war front and quite a number of the Italian ships surrendered to some of our guys in the Royal Navy. The captured ships were brought round into St Paul's Bay to anchor. My opinion was that these 'enemy' sailors had had enough of the war and just wanted out of the way of it. Ironically, I found myself admiring the lovely lines of their cruisers, but, evidently, they were not crewed by men with hearts to fight and who would do what was asked of them and so their ships were of limited value to them.

Meanwhile, our priority was still the repair of our own ship and so we set out from Malta to a port called Taranto, just at the very south of Italy. There was a dry dock in which the ship could be repaired. Sadly, there were one or two incidents of men behaving badly. That led to other difficulties and here is why.

When a ship the size of ours is in dry dock, moving off the ship is hazardous. Our route was via a gangplank, but it was fairly narrow with only a single rope on each side to prevent a serious fall. There was no great stability about the gangplank and, if anyone had fallen off, they would certainly have met their death because the bottom of the dry dock was so far below. That did not deter men going ashore and getting drunk, thereby being totally ill-equipped for the dangers encountered coming back onto the ship via the dry dock.

Our solution was to arrange for a few people who were on duty to be on the other side of the gangplank to make sure the men were escorted and taken safely on to the ship That worked well for some of the men returning, but when you had someone who was fairly 'well-oiled' and could not have walked in a straight line even if you had given them a thousand pounds to do so, we had to be inventive. On one or two occasions, we had to sock the guy on the chin, knock him out and then lift him on board as it was too dangerous to risk the alternative.

Eventually the ship was repaired and we made our way from the dry dock to another port called Brindisi on Italy's south eastern coast. It was also an interesting place. For one thing, the Air Force had a base there and, indeed, from time to time we entertained some of the RAF personnel. They, in turn, invited some of us out to the airfield from which they were operating and, on one memorable occasion, I was taken up in a Lockheed Hudson bomber along with one or two friends. They put me in the forward turret.

For the vast majority of you who do not know the design of this aircraft, let me explain that there was a turret in the front where the forward gunner was located with all the other fellas seated in other parts of the plane. I tell you I was never so frightened in all my life. We took off over the sea and there I was, feeling like a vulnerable spare part, totally on my own and with no contact with the rest of the folks on the plane. I was glad, overjoyed and ecstatic just to get out of that plane and vowed I would never ever do such a thing again.

SIX : *In Search of a Brother*

During our stay in Brindisi, I was blessed by the most amazing experience involving a reunion with my elder brother Jim who had enlisted in the Army in the very early stages of the war in 1939. Jim was a hero to younger brother George and myself, particularly because, while we were still at school, he had gone away to war and had been through all of the North African campaign. He had experienced action in the desert, had been reported missing twice and had been mentioned in despatches on at least one occasion.

The Kirkland family on the evening of Jim's departure to war

Everywhere I went, I would enquire as to where his 316 company of the RASC (Royal Army Service Corps) was based. In Brindisi, there was an Army HQ for that area and I visited there to enquire about the whereabouts of this company. The sergeant at the desk was not able to help me, but another soldier was passing by and, noticing my naval uniform, he asked what I was looking for. I told him I was trying to find my brother. On mention of his name he said, "Oh Jimmy Kirkland? I know him"` and he told me where to find him. Imagine the thrilling prospect of meeting a member of your family so many miles from home in the middle of a war!

Since there was a bit of travel involved, to make it a reality, I had to make a request to my skipper to have time off to try to locate my brother. However, moving around in a time of war has its own special challenges and it was no simple matter to get to Bari, which was the nearest large area to where Jim was. As I went ashore from my own ship, there were people who had been caught up in the bombing in Bari the night before. It was a most horrible sight to see the bodies, all of them blackened and charred, whether alive or dead. Such were the awful consequences of the burns they had experienced. Before leaving for Bari, several of us had to spend an hour or so helping to remove these bodies from the ships as they came alongside.

Eventually, I was cleared to leave and went to Bari in the company of an officer. We travelled by jeep a distance of about seventy miles up the coast, which had been bombed pretty badly the night before, and there was smoke still rising from the harbour area.

When we arrived in Bari, I had to report to General Alexander's Headquarters to enquire as to how I was going to see my brother. Arrangements were soon made. I was told that there would be a despatch rider put at my disposal to take me out to a little village call Valenzano, where Jim's company was located. I arrived on the pillion of the motorbike. His company at that time was billeted in a monastery in front of which was a parade ground where the sentry was and I enquired of him about Sergeant James Kirkland. There was not another person around. It was so quiet and still in the middle of the countryside. Pointing to a nearby doorway, he uttered the words that I longed to hear: "Sergeant Kirkland is over there". Jim was actually duty sergeant that day. Imagine his surprise on seeing a sailor, miles from the sea, walking across the parade ground. He came towards me. I recognised him, but he had no idea that he was moving towards his little brother. It was not until we were two or three yards away from each other that he realised who had appeared in front of him. I had still been at school when he left home.

Brothers reunited

There was a tremendous reunion. He got leave for the rest of the day and we spent it in Bari. It was mid summer and very hot. We wondered where we could go that might give us some reasonable privacy to talk after so many years and that would also offer shelter from the sun. The only viable option was a cinema. As you can imagine, we did not see anything that was being shown. I had to provide answers to all the questions he had about mum and dad and Margaret (his girlfriend) and so many other items of news. It was really an exciting time. All too soon, I had to take my leave of him and get back to the ship. Jim arranged for me to get a lift in a form of transport nicknamed a 'big mac'. This was a massive tank transporter. The driver was able to take me within about two or three miles of Brindisi but, at that point, he had to divert and go elsewhere so I walked the rest of the way into Brindisi.

Suddenly, reality dawned on me. Here was I, walking along a fairly quiet road in Navy uniform, in a foreign country with which we were at war! It gave me quite a shock to realise the danger lurking in this place. However, I managed to get back on board the ship and was delighted to have met up with Jim. He later came down to Brindisi and visited the ship and, once again, it was a special pleasure to be in the company of my brother after so many years apart.

SEVEN : *To the Wider World*

From Italy we sailed east on the Mediterranean towards Lebanon and its capital Beirut. From the sea, the city – often referred to as the 'Paris of the East' - appeared so affluent with its grand, imposing seafront but the impressive frontage belied the poverty concealed behind. This was the picture in so many different ports which we visited.

Our task was to transfer some cargo from Beirut to Malta, but out there in the Mediterranean sea there were dangers lurking in the form of enemy submarines. A decision was taken to delay sailing until the weather became stormy thus making it more difficult for submarines to operate. In the interim, the men were given an opportunity to go over to nearby Damascus, a short bus trip over the mountains. Imagine my grief when I was prevented from going on the trip. I had misbehaved around that time and was therefore not allowed to go. I still feel the pain of that, particularly since I have never had the opportunity to visit Damascus.

After a delay of about two weeks in Beirut, the weather did worsen and, feeling a little less apprehensive about the hostile submarines in the bay, we were able to move out and sail towards Malta. During the second day at sea, the weather became more violent than anything we had ever experienced before. Truly, I sympathised with the experience of St Paul as he headed for Rome and was shipwrecked en route. We experienced our own fatalities. On that hazardous

trip, we lost two ratings, two men over the side, blown away without there being anything we could do about retrieving them. That was a devastating situation and a poignant reminder of our vulnerability.

We arrived in Malta, but the weather had been so severe that the fo'c'sle (the forecastle or forward part of the ship) had been damaged and so, once again, we had to be sidelined for repairs.

Thereafter, the adventure continued with a posting to Port Said in Egypt where we remained for quite a number of months. I remember Port Said very well because, from there, we used to have to go down through the Suez Canal after

Ashore at Port Said

which we would enter the 'Bitter Lakes' which open out after the narrow pass of the canal itself. I always remember the skipper announcing through the ship's intercom that if we looked over on the port side we would see where Moses got the KRs and AIs. Now for those who were not in the Navy and did not know what he was telling us, the KRs and AIs are the Kings Rules and Admiralty Instructions. He was pointing out that this was where Moses got his instructions from the Lord on Mount Sinai.

On one of our trips through the canal, we had to proceed down into East Africa carrying a shipload of bananas on the upper deck. We had been told to take these down into a port in Masawa which was in Eritrea in East Africa. Whereas nowadays we accept without surprise many different colours of skin on our streets, in those days I had no previous direct encounter with black people. It was very surprising to me to see so many black people on the jetty as we tied up the liberty boat (so called) that transferred us from our ship, anchored in the harbour, to the shore.

But there was something else that arrested my attention and caused me even more surprise. There was big girder sticking out of the side of the jetty and, to my amazement, on it were painted the words 'Colville's Ltd, Dalziel', the very place where I had been working as a boy. This was steel they had produced long before I had worked there. It was so interesting seeing a girder made in Motherwell at Dalziel Steelworks firmly installed in East Africa.

Unfortunately, honesty forces me to recount that once again in this port my behaviour was of a questionable standard. One day, coming back on the liberty boat, I landed over the side on account of my antics and bad behaviour and had to be fished out of the water. That was bad enough, but when I got back on board my leave was stopped. Since we were going to be in Masawa for a few days, the other guys were allowed to go up into the mountains to Asmara and I missed out on that, but at least I learned one big lesson!

While most of the guys were on shore, the ship was fairly quiet and I remember being at the stern, just feeling quite sorry for myself, when all of a sudden there was a great commotion in the water. I dashed over to look and could see many fish moving about in desperate fashion. The cause was also very obvious: two enormous sharks were creating havoc among the rest of the marine life in the harbour. I tell you, I will never ever forget that scene; it was spine chilling. Although it was a very warm day, I began to shiver and shake when I realised I had been in that harbour the night before. So that was a very scary experience but I think it might have contributed very positively to keeping my later behaviour in check.

The time came for us to leave Masawa and return to Alexandria in Egypt. By that point, the army and our forces had been moving well up through Italy and, consequently, it was a lot quieter in the Mediterranean theatre of war.

Alexandria 1944

Having volunteered, I was subsequently offered the opportunity to go through for a commission in the Royal Navy but for this I had to leave my ship in Alexandria and come back to the UK. On being put ashore, I had to make my way to the transit camp on the edge of the desert just outside Alexandria. I was totally inexperienced in the necessary survival techniques. Although I was given a bed to lie on, I tell you that was possibly the worst night ever in my life because I was seriously bitten by bugs. In the end, I crawled over to the toilet where I think I collapsed before wakening up in hospital. I do not really know how serious it was; I do not even remember being carried on a stretcher onto the ship that was to transport me home and the first few days of the voyage on HMS Durban Castle were spent in the sick bay.

Having made some form of recovery, I was just in time to encounter the travails of sailing through the Bay of Biscay, a very treacherous and tempestuous stretch of water. The conditions we faced were close to mountaineering. As we climbed the waves, it was as if we were looking up at Mount Everest. A moment or two later, we were looking down into a deep watery ravine. People who have never been to sea do not realise the frightening experience of being in really rough seas. However, we survived and eventually were overjoyed to find ourselves entering the Clyde estuary.

I was amazed, having been in all these arid places, to see the foliage, the green trees and fields. It was so refreshing. It was very early in the morning and I remember being up on the deck, tears streaming down my cheeks, as we sailed back into Scotland. I was glad to be back.

When I left the troop ship at Greenock, I only had to cross over the Clyde to Dunoon once again to my base at HMS Osprey. I spent about two months there brushing up on my anti-submarine detection information, but was able to get home on quite a number of weekends. Actually, it was quite embarrassing. Here was I, supposedly in the Navy, but appearing home from time to time. I remember on one occasion, while still at Dunoon, arranging a pass to take me to London so that I would not be embarrassed by folks seeing me so much on home territory. That was my mindset at the time.

From HMS Osprey I was posted south to Harwich to join a ship called HMS Mackay. This was a clan class destroyer, built around the late 1920s. Though quite an old ship, it was in good shape. The job that we had to do at that time was running out of Harwich to escort ships that were leaving the south of England bound for Archangel and Murmansk. We escorted some of these convoys right up past the north of Scotland to Norway before we turned back.

On the return leg, we would escort other ships that were returning from the Russian ports away up in the artic circle. Many a time on that route we had to run the gauntlet of German E boats. They were similar to our MTB's - motor torpedo boats. I remember that we had to be so careful at sea because ships had to sail along sea lanes that had been swept for mines. The lanes were marked with buoys and one of the ploys that the E boats had was to tie up at one of them. They would sit there unable to be picked up by our radar. With their engines on silent, they were easily confused on our radar screens with marker buoys. Think, too, about the pitch black nights in the North Sea. It was only when the convoys were alongside that they could recognise the E-boats, but by then it could be too late. The enemy at that point could very easily pick off one or two of the ships in the convoy with their torpedoes.

This was a dangerous assignment but the E boats did not have it all their own way. On one occasion we sank one of their E boats and had to pick up their crew out of the water. Well I can remember these men being lined up on the stern deck of our ship and our captain coming down to inspect and address them. A horrible thing happened. One of the Germans spat at our skipper as he passed. That was shocking behaviour and we were very annoyed and angry with those prisoners of war. I will not tell you just exactly what happened to those people, but in future, I learned that our new policy was not to pick up any more survivors in such a situation.

On a more positive note, a shipmate, inspired by our bravado, penned the following lines.

THE VETERAN FIVE

You've heard the tale of the Light Brigade
Of the mad yet glorious charge they made
But, have you heard the one of the sea
When five old destroyers tackled the mighty three
Braved bombs, and mines, and eleven inch shells
As they steamed thro the North Sea's surging swells
And faltered not nor hesitated
When the pride of the German fleet they baited
The Scharnhorst, Gneisenua and Prince Eugen
Manned by the "Vaterlands" bravest men.
They called them old and obsolete
These veterans of the last war fleet
Yet when the call to action came
They proved that they still knew the game
And tho they failed to sink the hun
They surely earned the words "WELL DONE"

During the time when we were in harbour at Harwich, we used to see and hear the flying bombs launched from the continent and bound for London. It was very disconcerting to hear them. However, in one sense, 'hearing them' was a little consoling because we knew that it was when they switched off that they were ready to drop their terrible cargo. London was on the receiving end of so many of these bombs and it was such a scary time.

Meanwhile my intention of training for a commission had met a serious snag. I realised that, to complete my ambition, I had to sign on for an additional two years. I had not understood that and so opted out. However, while still on HMS Mackay, and in consideration of my experience, and my record in the Navy, I was put in charge of a group of young men who were training to be officers. They were good quality material and I helped them to develop their seamanship and taught them various things they had to learn about life on board ship.

EIGHT : *Honoured Service*

Although there had been times in the Navy when I had not been particularly proud of my record of behaviour, some qualities must have shone through, because just as the war concluded, I was chosen to be the bodyguard of the Commander-in-Chief. He was a Vice Admiral and had a tremendous record during the war.

Several interesting things happened while I was looking after the Commander-in-Chief. One of these was attending hearings of people who had been associated with Quisling – the crime of helping the enemy. We were visiting a prison where the accused were housed and there I saw some things that I did not particularly enjoy. One, for instance, involved a lovely blonde girl who had been living with some of the Germans. She was being held in prison and, because she would not answer the questions that were put to her by the guards, she was given a few slaps across the face. I felt quite sorry for her but assumed it must have been necessary at that time.

A more pleasant memory is that, along with other members of the crew, I visited the home of Greig, the great Norwegian composer. We saw his piano and heard it being played. This was a pleasant distraction from all that had been happening earlier on. We proceeded to Trondheim where a victory parade had been arranged and, of course, I was involved in that with my Commander-in-Chief.

The parade ended in Trondheim Cathedral but, because I was wearing side arms at the time, I was not allowed to go into the sanctuary. While I was standing in the wings, the verger started to speak to me. His English was not very good; my Norwegian was non-existent, but somehow I must have managed to communicate that my father was a sculptor. I believe this guy thought that I must have been from the Michelangelo family because he started to show me all the finer points of the building! I had to be careful that I did not lose sight of the man I was supposed to be looking after! After the parade finished, we were taken to the Britannia Hotel in Trondheim along with other senior officers. Such were the gracious qualities of my Commander-in-Chief that when we went to the hotel, he would not sit down until he knew that I was being served. I was impressed by his concern. The parade brought together the senior person in the Army and the senior person in the Royal Air Force. It turned out that the senior member of the Royal Air Force personnel was Maxwell Riddell from

Motherwell. I think, at that time, he may have been a Squadron Leader. He had been in the Royal Air Force before the war as a regular but had clearly progressed to the top. While I was in Norway, I really fell in love with that country, its fantastic scenery, and its charming people.

Arriving in Norway

One of the things that touched me very much was the fact that, during the war years, they never had the experience of eating meat; they had to live on fish during the entire time of the German occupation. On board ship we developed the habit of keeping scraps of food that had been left over while we were at sea. When we came into harbour, young Norwegians would be invited on board and given a good meal. It was humbling to see those quality young people attacking that meal as if they had not seen meat before. We enjoyed good relationships with these young Norwegians and used to go ashore and walk with them.

Being greeted by the Norwegians

It was at that time that I experienced the grandeur of being in the land of the midnight sun. In the middle of June, and even beyond, the sun was still in the sky well after midnight and it was just a wonderful experience.

Some time later, I received a very special gift - a plaque signed by King Olav of Norway for services to the Norwegian people. I believe it was because I had the privileged position of looking after the Commander-in-Chief. I was also thrilled to receive a special scroll thanking me for my participation in the liberation of the Norwegian people.

THE LIBERATION OF NORWAY 8th MAY 1945

THE PEOPLE OF NORWAY WISH TO THANK YOU

Wallace J Kirkland

OF THE BRITISH ARMED FORCES
FOR YOUR VALUABLE SERVICES IN
HELPING TO RESTORE FREEDOM
TO OUR LAND

OSLO, DECEMBER 1945.

Many years later, and on a number of occasions, I was delighted to return to Norway in the company of some young Scots, this time for holiday purposes.

On return from service in Norway, I was posted back to Devonport on HMS Drake. This brought me close to the home of the Bellechamber and Hill families but, sadly, I did not choose to re-connect with them. Since I had last been in contact, I had more or less forsaken Christian things and had certainly abandoned the devotional times which had sustained me spiritually in those early Navy days. By now, I had more fondness for other attractions.

I say that to my shame, but there are always lessons to learn from the times that we fail. No wonder scripture advises: "If a man thinketh he standeth, take care lest he fall". Time after time, we are shown, both in scripture and in our own experience, how our relationship with God can fluctuate. A time when we feel the warmth of His presence in our lives can so quickly be followed by a period in the icy cold of rebellion.

Being away from home, I was able to involve myself in all the hitherto 'no-go' areas of life without anyone being around to keep me in check (or so I thought). This is typical of so many young people nowadays and was certainly the case then. Sometimes, their parents and other church members are unaware of their prodigality.

As I look back and see God's hand in my life during those years away, I realise how important it has been to me to be part of a process of keeping young people from being spiritually shipwrecked. Sadly, we often have to battle as hard as we do because the church does not seem to be able to attract and involve them in forms of service that they find meaningful and so they can become totally detached.

After one month at Devonport, I was transferred to HMS Onslaught, a destroyer, on which I completed my service. My final experience was on patrol in the North Sea.

During my last months on HMS Onslaught, I was able to take leave and come home because my brother Jim had returned from Italy and was going to be married to his long time fiancée, Margaret Gemmell. That was quite an occasion. However, brother Jim was never a flatterer and I remember him making remarks about my underwear! In the Navy, when you were out on patrol on the cold, cold waters, we used to have 'long johns' as they were called. They were coloured pink and he ribbed me about this - something about which I took a dim view.

Within a short time, I left the Navy and for that I was grateful. When demobbed from any of the services, one was kitted out with everything: shoes, socks, underwear and suit. I always remember I had a soft hat as well. I was so anxious to get out of the Navy at that particular time. I took the suit even though it did not fit me particularly well. Someone else would get the benefit of it but it certainly was not going to be me. But it was great to get back home!

And now for something important that I have not yet told you. During all the time I had been in the Navy, I had been corresponding with Nettie, this girlfriend of mine whom I had met in Colville's office. Nettie always kept the letters and, on one occasion, I remember the children discovering them, thereby getting to know just how much their mum meant to me during my Navy career – an unforgettable chapter in a full and interesting life.

NINE : *Married With Children*

Our Wedding   Photograph by Sharp of Hamilton

After my demob from the Navy, it did not take me long to get better acquainted with Nettie Robertson, to whom I had been writing so passionately all of the time I had been away. Most of our courting had been done by letter.

Nettie was the fourth of five girls in the Robertson family - James and Barbara Robertson being her parents. Mr Robertson was an insurance agent with the Co-operative Insurance Company and a very devout Christian. He was also very well respected among his clients and neighbours alike. The whole family attended Burnbank Methodist Church (where Nettie and I were to be married in March 1947).

Nettie was the only one in the family who went to music lessons and, on her twelfth birthday, her father took her to Cuthbertson's music shop in Glasgow where he bought her a fine upright piano.

Treasured possession

This was to become one of Nettie's treasured possessions and it always graced our home throughout our married life which, sadly, was brought to a conclusion on 7 March 2002. It was a sad day when I had to dispose of the piano, knowing that Nettie had enjoyed playing it so much. Unfortunately, owing to the piano having been subjected to central heating over many years, I was advised, not least of all by my good friend Peter Jackson (blind pianist and piano tuner), that the piano could not be properly tuned anymore.

One particularly warm memory I have of Nettie was when she was the church organist. I regularly attended their evening services. However, I cannot remember listening to the minister and what he had to say for Nettie's playing was what I enjoyed most.

As I look back on my singing days I realise Nettie very seldom played for me in public. She was always very critical of me in my timing, saying "You take your time from the town clock rather than the music"! The only retort I could think of was that I was the soloist and she was the accompanist and she had to follow me!! She taught me a whole lot.

Wedded bliss   Photograph by Sharp of Hamilton

Soon it became clear that Nettie and I wished to be married and spend the rest of our lives together, but first there was the small matter of getting a job!

After I left the Royal Navy in 1946, I was quite clear that I did not want to go back to Colville's to be stuck in an office day after day. Both my brothers, Jim and George, were involved by this time in the family's monumental sculptor business and my dad thought that to have three of us there would be just too congested!

However, anxious to see me settled into a job, father bought a piece of ground in Allanton near Shotts. This was a nursery with a big walled garden and was part of a very large estate. And so I settled down to work there enjoying the scope offered by the job and the opportunity to spend time out of doors.

The day came (22 March 1947) when Nettie and I were joined together in holy matrimony! Initially, we lived with my grandmother in Burnbank at 11 William Street. Nettie's mother lived only fifty or sixty yards away and back to back with my grandmother at 92 Dalzell Street. We had the use of one bedroom, one living room and the kitchen and the amount we paid at that time to my granny was two pounds per week. That included quite a lot of extras, not least of all my granny cooking for us. Looking back this was quite a special time.

I remember the first car I had was a Lee Francis. The registration number was RV 1959. The two rear doors had a tendency to stay open so they had to be tied together to keep them shut! The car was far from being a good starter. To allow for this, every time I came home, I turned the car at the top of the street so that it was facing down hill so that early in the morning I could get a good start. My daily journey was a distance of ten miles to Allanton and, if my memory serves me right, apart from those little snags with the doors and initial starting problems, the car never let me down.

On account of my dad's faith in me, I was determined to succeed in business and so enrolled for night classes in horticulture at the West of Scotland Agricultural College in Glasgow.

I suppose the determination to do well is a useful quality and one which is well supported in scripture: "Whatever your hand finds to do, do it with all your might". This should be an antidote to any feelings of lethargy we feel about tasks that we have been given to do.

If life was progressing well in terms of my profession, there was stalemate, spiritually speaking. Sadly, the Navy legacy had been to stifle my desire for Christian things and I was not at all interested in going to church services. However, fortunately Nettie had a more sincere and active faith than I and she was enthusiastic about attending church, so we made our way to Ebenezer Brethren Church in Pollock Street in Burnbank. What amazed me about this place was the singing. It was tremendous – and that despite there being neither organ nor piano! Such quality praise, of course, immediately connected with my personal interest in singing. Also attending this church were friends who had known my mum and dad for quite some time - Duncan and May Ferguson. They were very kind to us and invited us to their house on a Sunday evening. Their lovely home was called Fullwood House and was tied to the Fullwood Foundry next door. Mr Ferguson had a top job in Colville's Ltd, later to become British Steel. Nettie would play the piano and they would ask me to sing.

When I look back, I thank God for that time in my life. I was not interested in Christian things, but Christians were interested in me and I was so impressed that they would go to the trouble of entertaining us on a Sunday. I see that experience as one of the major steps in my return to committing my life to the Lord. Incidentally, at the time of writing I still visit Mrs Ferguson who is now well into her 90s.

Let me encourage you, following the example of the Fergusons, never to lose interest in the sheep that have gone astray. Continue to care for them and it may be that your love will be instrumental in bringing them back.

Meanwhile, Nettie and I began to consider a house move closer to my place of work at Allanton and so began a house hunt in the local area. In the circumstances, Wishaw appeared to meet all the criteria and, after a short time, we found that there was a house for sale there in the town's Mossneuk Crescent, number 49.

Nettie and my mother had gone to see the house and thought it would be ideal for us. It was left to my father and me to "seal the deal". The lady who was selling the house was a very fine Christian. On arrival, I could scarcely believe the name of the house: Ebenezer. I had been brought up in Motherwell and had attended Ebenezer Hall and there was the prospect of my coming to Wishaw to live in a house with the same name! If you are assuming I was pleased, you are very wrong. This was an embarrassment. I just felt this was not the kind of name I would put on a house, particularly in my spiritual state. However, the house was attractive and so eagerly we began the process of trying to buy it. The asking price for "Ebenezer" was sixteen hundred pounds. To our dismay, the owner told us that there had been a prior offer of seventeen hundred pounds! My father's quick response was that his son was also prepared to offer seventeen hundred pounds. He did not realise the challenge that he was creating because, at that time, my take-home pay was £4.15s.1d. (approximately £4.75). Nettie was earning two pounds per week in the flower shop. (She was a florist and worked with my sister in Motherwell.) And so we bought "Ebenezer" - but I had to take on a mortgage. There were no big Halifax offices, or similar, where you could easily arrange automated monthly payments as one can now. I had to go to a lawyer's office to make my monthly payment in cash. The same houses today, incidentally, would be valued around ninety thousand to ninety-five thousand pounds - quite a difference.

When we arrived in Wishaw, I did not fully realise that we were only about one hundred yards away from Alex and Jean Lochhead. That was a bit of a problem for me as they were very keen Christians and I was not.

Lifelong friends: Alex and Jean Lochhead

Alex was a friend of my brother Jim and this was the bad news, for I sensed he would pressurise me about spiritual things. However, I thank God on every remembrance of Alex because, in spite of the rebuffs I gave him over a number of months, he would come to our back door of an evening with the announcement that "this is the prayer meeting tonight, Wallace". Of course, I was not the least interested in prayer meetings, but how he kept coming and coming! It must have been totally of the Lord. As I look back on my life, the persistence of Alex and Jean Lochhead is a highly significant factor in my spiritual development. The Lochheads became our closest friends over all the years. Although Alex died a number of years ago, I still keep in touch with Jean.

Ultimately Alex's persistence paid off. His burden was 'to do something' with young people. He was starting a youth fellowship and wanted me to help him. Alex had worn me down and I did, indeed, agree to help. It was one of the most important decisions of my life. So many of the young people that were involved in the youth fellowship at that time became very fine friends. I thank God for all that happened during these early days at Wishaw and for 'Ebenezer' at 49 Mossneuk Crescent. We never did change the house name.

Although Mossneuk Park is now surrounded by other housing developments, in our early days living there we had farmers' fields behind us. The cows used to graze in the field and I well remember one morning being awakened by the noise of cattle seemingly a bit closer than normal. They had broken through the fence and were grazing in our back garden. Picture the scene: Wallace running around Mossneuk Crescent trying to herd up the cows and return them to the field just after five o'clock in the morning. It must have been quite a sight.

By the time we had been married for the best part of five years, we were expecting our first child. I was fortunate to have an aunt and uncle, Tom & Margaret Johnstone, who stayed at number 10 Mossneuk Crescent. How grateful we should be for the support of family and friends. They were on constant alert as the time drew near to take Nettie to hospital. When Nettie's time came, I did what had been suggested: I telephoned Tom Johnstone and he took Nettie to the maternity hospital at Motherwell - and I went back to bed! Normally, I would have been up at half past six, but I think I wakened that morning around eight o'clock. When I telephoned the hospital, Barbara had already been born. I was a bit slack in not being more attentive and I felt a wee bit ashamed.

Barbara was born in 1952 and, three years later, the boys arrived, Archie and Jimmy. This was something else! I remember taking Barbara with me when I went to collect her mum and the twins from hospital.

Jimmy and Archie

Nettie had been anxious about being away from Barbara while in hospital but, when we arrived there, Barbara could not have cared less about mum or the boys. She just wandered around nosing into everything she could see. (She hasn't changed!) I think Nettie was a little upset that Barbara hadn't come rushing up to her with outstretched arms, but that is just the way it was.

The arrival of the twins prompted us to look for alternative accommodation because we had to find more space and so eventually we moved from Wishaw to 96 Manse Road, Motherwell. I had known the previous owners of this house from the time I had lived in Manse Road as a boy. The family name was Lamb, two brothers and a sister. They had a haulage contractors business. I always remember the big red lorries sitting at the side of this house. Our new home suited us very well and, once again, we were grateful to Alex Lochhead who, on account of his acquaintance with the owners, helped us acquire it.

Nettie and I enjoyed the time that we spent at 96 Manse Road and, at that time, we attended Ebenezer Gospel Hall in Motherwell. I later became Bible Class leader there.

Now we are five!

One incident that sticks out in my mind about that house in Manse Road took place when the children were small. I had bought an electric hedge cutter to help me control the very large surrounding hedge which needed a lot of attention. I used to take some time off during the day just to keep the garden in order. One early evening, Nettie had put the children to bed. I was working outside and, before visiting her mother, she came out to see me. I had been working with the hedge cutter during a time when there had been a little smir of rain. It was not the best time to have been doing this work with an electric hedge cutter, but I was anxious to get the job done. After a short conversation, Nettie moved off and I started up the cutter again. Probably because of the dampness there was a short through my left hand and I was flung to the ground. That part of the garden was full of rose bushes and I was being thrown around trying all the time to free myself from the cutter. Nettie had seen this and, of course, was in panic. I had led the cable through the window of the front room and she had to go all the way into the house before she could remove the plug. During that time, the electrical current continued to cause me to writhe around. I understand that my colour was totally blue when the power was switched off. The wonderful thing was that within two or three minutes I was being attended by three doctors who stayed nearby. I remember my brother Jim coming to see me and, because of the shock, I was crying most of the time, but I thank God for that wake-up call that helped me see how quite easily one can not only be 'knocked out', but 'taken out' altogether. What a shock of a different kind to realise the awful possibility of having gone straight into eternity from a life that was not right with God. The message about our vulnerability and the brevity of time is clear.

We enjoyed our time living in Manse Road as well as developing the nursery. But perhaps more importantly there was a spiritual movement in my life at that time which I believe led later to more focused activity for God.

TEN : *Developing In Business*

I was a novice market gardener and was grateful to people who helped me. In particular, there was Matt Aikman, who lived on the other side of the Clyde Valley and travelled over with other helpers, among them, a young man named James Good. During that time, he made a great impact on my life. He was a genuine, hard-working man and a very strong Christian. That was one thing I was not, having been in the Navy and away from the Christian influence for a very long time; my life had gone a bit 'agley'. I remember the influence that young man had. He often encouraged me to sing hymns with him, particularly at lunchtime. Even when we were working together, he would quote scriptures. I look back on that time with a great deal of joy and thankfulness. Throughout my whole life, God has brought people into my life who have been a great challenge and encouragement to me.

However, market gardening was hard and I was not convinced that we were getting the fruit of our labours. Increasingly, I believed that if we were growing the crops, then we should get the benefit of any profit that was to be had. Too much of the available profit was being absorbed by the middlemen in the market. So it was determined that we should open a shop in Wishaw. That shop at 203 Main Street I will always remember. It had two large windows facing onto the main thoroughfare but, on initial inspection, the interior of the shop was deeply depressing. There was a great deal of remedial work to be done before we could get involved in trading. In fact, you would have broken your leg if you had walked too far through from the front to the back. However, the determining factor was that, having worked for a whole year in the nursery, we had made just under a hundred pounds profit which, in anybody's language, was totally inadequate for the work and finance expended on running the place.

The shop soon began to take shape and we began to sell our own produce. At the time, I remember being intrigued by an advert from another firm who had a nursery and shops. They used the slogan: **"We Grow – We Sell"**. Some wit changed that to: **"We Grow – We Smell"**.

Whether we grew produce effectively or not is for others to judge, but I do know we worked hard on those premises in which we were able to sell much of our own produce: lettuce, tomatoes, flowers. However, naturally there was still a substantial amount of produce that had to be bought from the market.

On the other hand, if we had an oversupply of our own produce, we would take it to the market for sale.

The work in the shop, while rewarding, was very hard. The hours were long and we had to be up and running by about 5am so as to get into the market in time to be back for the shop opening. It seemed a long time until lunch at which point I got home for a bite to eat. I soon learned to take a rest for about half an hour and then be back on duty until the end of the working day which was about 9pm. At the weekends, we finished even later, but it all proved to be quite rewarding. Latterly, at weekends, we had sixteen people working in the shop. However, major competition was on the horizon.

Supermarkets were just becoming the 'in thing' and people were encouraged to make that their one-stop-shop. I tried to copy that for a wee while and set out produce in supermarket style, but, in the end, took cold feet. I realise now that I should have kept that going in order to ensure we always had people coming in.

Not content with the shop and the busyness of work, I discovered that there was a potato merchant locally who was retiring and we were able to buy that business. It was Thomas Tennent, Potato Merchants of Russell Street in Wishaw. That enabled us not only to bring in potatoes from the growers in various parts of the country, but also to start wholesaling them around the shops and, of course, we included our fruit and vegetables and other produce and so we had expanded to become a wholesale fruit and potato merchant at that time.

Some years later, we also opened fruit shops in Motherwell and Bellshill. Nettie, being a florist, made a great contribution within the shops. However, meantime there were interesting developments on other fronts.

ELEVEN : _Inspired By Evangelism_

In 1955, Billy Graham came to head up what became known as the All Scotland Crusade. He preached for eight weeks in the Kelvin Hall, Glasgow to packed audiences. Thousands came to faith and Scotland has benefited ever since. The gospel was surely demonstrated to be Good News. The Crusade certainly had an impact on my life.

Its beginning had seen me still cool about Christian things, though my friend, Alex Lochhead, was trained as a counsellor. At first, I intended to keep my distance, but it was exciting to hear of all the preparations that were being made. I was very impressed. I guess one of the things that fascinated me was to think of the people behind this: who invited this preacher with tremendous ability? I never considered myself to be a front man, but being behind influential events still excites my imagination.

On a Saturday evening prior to the commencement of the Crusade evenings, there was an event for counsellors. My friend, Alex Lochhead, was unable to attend and I took his ticket. That was the first time I saw and heard Mr Graham preach. He was good looking, only in his late thirties and spoke with power and absolute conviction.

No-one could remain unmoved by what happened next: people were coming to faith; churches were being filled and, to this day, there are Christians making an impact on account of their putting faith in Jesus Christ at the All Scotland Crusade. Of course, as anyone with insight would tell you, the preacher is only really the spearhead and the figurehead. Mass evangelism works when individuals catch the vision and bring their friends under the sound of the preaching of the gospel.

Billy Graham had been invited to Scotland by ministers who were part of the 'Tell Scotland' Crusade. Some of those ministers known to me were the Reverends Tom Allan, Ian Doyle and Peter Bissett. They had heard Mr Graham preach in London's Earls Court. The thing that impressed me most was that they did not invite him merely for one week or a fortnight, but for several weeks - to the twenty thousand seater Kelvin Hall. The Crusade, in the end, lasted eight weeks in all! Such faith by these men was greatly rewarded as, night by night, the Kelvin Hall was full to overflowing. On the last night, there were more people outside the hall than inside! Mr Graham even took time to speak to these people outside.

The reason it is so important to mention this is because of the impact it had in my life. To witness the faith of these men being honoured by God in such a mighty way was a turning point for me.

I am so reminded of the incident in the gospels in which four friends carried the paralytic man to Jesus, reaching Him by lowering the bed through the roof of the house. We read that Jesus referred to the *faith of those friends*, not specifically the faith of the man on the bed. When I think of the faith of those who arranged those weeks of meetings in Kelvin Hall so that others could meet Jesus, I see the connection with that miracle in scripture.

All of our lives are impacted by prior experiences during which seeds are sown and, in some cases, visions are planted. It was like that for me during that event in 1955. Although I would not have necessarily understood it in these terms at the time, I was aspiring to be like those who brought the paralytic man on the bed; I wanted to be a catalyst in making things happen.

Billy Graham had preached at Earls Court in the previous year, 1954, and, not surprisingly, a key issue for Christian leaders throughout the UK was how to follow up what had been established. That would involve not only keeping some momentum going, but helping with the spiritual feeding process that was so necessary to build up spiritual strength across the nation. The gifts of the evangelist now had to be supplemented using the spiritual teaching gifts of others.

Among Christian leaders in London at that time was Lindsay Glegg whose vision was to have a week long Christian extravaganza that became known as "Filey", on account of the venue being at Butlins Holiday Camp at Filey in Yorkshire. Filey was an ideal location because it was pretty much equidistant between London and Glasgow, the two centres where Billy Graham had preached. I learned about Filey subsequent to the year it was established and Nettie and I, with our very young family, were regular attendees for the next seven or eight years.

The Filey Holiday Crusade, as it was called, was sponsored by MWE – 'Movement for World Evangelisation'. About six thousand people attended each year. There had never been anything quite like it. (Eventually, Filey gave way to contemporary conventions such as Spring Harvest).

The reason I emphasise the importance of Filey is because it had such an impact on my Christian experience. In some areas of management training these days, I believe they talk about the "Cascade Method" of training. That describes the situation in which the message 'cascades' from one person or group to another. What a wonderful picture of how the gospel and evangelism should operate across church and society. The whole thinking behind Filey was that six thousand attendees should go home and not merely be influenced within the confines of their own lives, but impact on other people.

The Bible teaching each morning was of the highest quality from such giants of the faith as Alan Redpath, Sidlaw Baxter, Herbert Cragg, Stephen Olford, George B Duncan and many more. I had only recently got my Christian experience back on track and I thank God for the Holy Spirit directing me into such a wonderful experience as this.

Looking back, what struck me was that when Christians of all persuasions come together under the ministry of God's Word, there is so much evidence of blessing. The Keswick Convention, held in July each year in Cumbria's Lake District, is another splendid example: Christians from all backgrounds meet under the banner "All One in Christ Jesus". Numbers are increasing each year. I was brought up in a Brethren Church and, perhaps as a consequence of its traditional independence, I was not used to being exposed to such interdenominational gatherings and teaching. What is especially interesting is to think that all of this might have been the catalyst for my desire to see all Christians working together, particularly in evangelism.

I have been greatly privileged to have been involved in a number of missions over the past forty years and I would like to put on record that I believe I have seen what God is pleased to do when a number of Christians come together to bring to the attention of their community the fact that, through faith in Jesus Christ, their lives and communities can be transformed. The basis for believing that is found in Holy Scriptures when they clearly communicate that Jesus Christ died on the cross for the sins of everyone; that he was buried and that he rose from the dead after three days. Active belief and faith in these events re-establishes our link with God. I wholeheartedly accept this as fact and it is my confidence in the historical reality of Jesus Christ, and my belief that the scriptural record of him is true, that fuels my enthusiasm even today.

However, passion and vision do not always rush into action and it was ten years later that I had my first experience of close involvement in the organisation of an evangelistic mission. Meanwhile, though I did not know it, I was on the verge of a form of Christian activity which was to be more or less a part of my life for at least the next fifty years.

TWELVE : *A Home for Maranatha*

By the time of the All Scotland Crusade, Alex Lochhead and I had been involved with the youth fellowship at Wishaw for more than a year, meeting on Thursday evenings. However, we began to feel uneasy about having contact with these young people restricted to only one hour a week. It was about this time that we started to think about the possibility of establishing a youth centre somewhere. This would enable us to be in touch with the young people in a more sustained way.

Alongside that fact was a realisation that although the folks in the churches were happy to see the young people there on a Sunday, they did not seem to appreciate that there were another six days in the week when their lives were not being touched by anything Christian.

The concept we had in mind was to have a place that could touch the lives of young people throughout the week. That was the germ of the idea that grew to become what we knew as the Maranatha Centre.

So began the search for suitable premises which, after a time, ultimately we found in Hope Street in Motherwell. The building had been an old knitting factory.

The old factory that became the Maranatha Centre

We purchased it for seven hundred and fifty pounds. None of us involved had too much money at that time but we were able to pay it in three separate instalments. Those involved right at the beginning were Sam Hill, Alex Lochhead, Bert Young, Robert Forrest, Willie Gunn, my brother George, Dan Ferguson, David Wilson and Billy Gilmour.

Acquiring the building from the previous owner was one thing, but having to clear the place of all the old machinery was quite another. I remember we had about three lorry loads of greasy old machines to clear out as well as their residue of dirt and grease on the floors. The place was so old. While we were scraping the walls to re-decorate, we discovered that there was a text on the wall. None of us could believe just what we were uncovering. The text stated: John 3.16: "For God so loved the world that He gave His only begotten Son that whosoever believeth in Him should not perish but have everlasting life". This was just mind-blowing at that particular time, because we had no knowledge of how the building had come to have such a text. On checking this out, we found that it had been the place of the original Town Mission in Motherwell and so would have been more than a hundred years old before we moved in.

It is so interesting to me that the street in which we were located was called Hope Street. I certainly felt that was appropriate for our Maranatha start-up. But it also brings to mind that in Hamilton, too, was a Hope Street and that was the venue for Hamilton Missionary Fellowship - brainchild of Jim Hyslop. I have always held all the folks that were involved in that work in very, very high esteem. They did a tremendous job with young people. Many are in fulltime service and on the mission field today through the work of the Hamilton Missionary Fellowship.

Whereas the role of HMF was directly missionary oriented, our work with young people was much more general and specifically concerned evangelism and helping to give young Christians a good grounding in their faith.

Early in 1956, after a lot of dedication and hard work, we were ready to convene our first evening in the newly established Maranatha Centre. The first event was for some of the people who had been helping with the renovations and some of our supporters. We were so proud of the place and of what had been established. I have one or two photographs of our Hope Street premises but, quite honestly, when I look at them now, I just do not understand how the young people were even attracted to such a place – but they were, and we thank God for that.

And so, miraculously, we were able to implement our plan to provide young people with a Christian environment available to them almost every night of the week. Each evening there was a different team of leaders. I had the responsibility for Mondays along with David Wilson and Bert Young; Alex Lochhead, accompanied by Robert Forrest, supervised on Tuesdays. Wednesday was when the younger children up to the age of twelve and thirteen were involved. Looking after them were Willie Gunn, George Kirkland and Dan Ferguson. Most importantly, on a Sunday evening, there was Youth Challenge. Friday evening was reserved for a different, but highly significant, activity: The Maranatha Choir practice. So many memories of that old building!

However it was not all plain sailing. Indeed, after we had got the place going, on several occasions the Centre was burgled. The leadership became convinced that those who were breaking in were some of the young people whom we were entertaining during part of the week. Eventually we bricked up the windows and it looked more like Fort Apache than a Christian Youth Centre.

But it was in this old building that so many lovely things happened. Many, many young people came to faith in the Lord Jesus and then they were encouraged to go on in their faith and were discipled by a range of others who gladly took that responsibility.

Building relationships with anyone, and particularly with young people, involves a willingness to be part of their lives whenever required. On at least one occasion, however, my offer of help seemed to exceed my competence. Here's the story. . .

There were three young fellows who stayed in the vicinity of the Maranatha Centre and on occasions I visited their home. Their mother was expecting another baby and I remember saying to her at that time, "If there is anything I can do, please don't be slow to telephone me" – and I left my telephone number. Quite some time after that, one night, well after midnight, I received a phone call telling me that Mrs Porter's waters had broken and, in the sleepy stupor I was in, I thought they had got the wrong number and that it was a plumber they were needing! You see I was not aware of "waters breaking" terminology heralding the birth of a child. It seems funny looking back, but, at the time, it was anything but!!

The Maranatha Centre always tried to cater for the needs of young people in at least three important areas: recreational, social and spiritual. Of course, the spiritual content was vital and we addressed spiritual needs in a variety of ways.

On a Monday evening we had Bible Studies in a little room called "the Quiet Room". Not being a Bible student or a Bible teacher myself, I opted to use the tapes of a well-known English preacher, the Rev Francis Dickson, from Landsdowne Baptist Church in Bournemouth. He issued study notes in conjunction with tapes and I used them to educate the group about the things of the Lord in a far better way than I could have done on my own. On a Tuesday night, Billy Gilmour and others were involved in the Bible Studies. Wednesday was a very special night for the youngsters who were encouraged in their faith in these early days.

A unique aspect of the Centre's ministry was the Maranatha Choir, formed one Friday evening in that building in Hope Street. It was started in connection with a Mission held in Carluke with Hedley Murphy. The choir began with about thirty-five to forty people - and quite a miscellaneous group of people they were, I remember!

The first person to take charge of the choir was Sam Hill. Then Peter Bennett became the conductor. Following on from him was Jim Law who was succeeded by Willie Kerr. The first pianist was Alistair Lochhead; then Alison Davidson who was followed by Esther Brooks (now Esther McColl). The choir did a sterling job for more than thirty-five years.

Special mention needs to be made of Youth Challenge held on Sunday evenings. In fact this was a legacy which pre-dated us going into the Maranatha Centre at Hope Street. The origin of Youth Challenge lay with a group of young men who included Bill Friel, Willie Wilding, Willie Hamilton, Jack Avril, Bert Amstrong, Alastair McGibbon and Currie Cunningham. These are the names I remember. Later on they were joined by John Jamieson and John Wright. John Jamieson became a minister in the Church of Scotland. In addition to the meetings themselves, Youth Challenge became synonymous with open-air meetings at what was known as Post Office Corner in Motherwell. Recall, or imagine, the scene: anything up to two hundred young people there witnessing, handing out gospel literature and singing gospel songs.

So much for the Centre's general pattern of activities, but there are some specific memories worth sharing as well - such as the night I asked John and Robert Pollock to leave because they were horsing around and had pulled down a curtain rail. I thought this was the end of the world and I asked them to leave. Their mother was on the phone to me for about an hour, really dressing me down for what I had done to her boys. Incidentally, those boys later became very good friends and if ever there was work needing done, John and Robert Pollock were two of the best workers around to do it.

As I survey the lives and development of so many young people whom we got to know through the Maranatha Centre, I have come to realise that it is not always the quiet and biddable young people who make the grade later on in life. Often, the young tearaways have an energy and a potential that is able to be channelled in very positive ways. (Some might consider me to be among their number!)

Being involved with young people gave us scope to develop even wider links with other youth groups and, in at least one case, those links were international. Betty Rankin, a missionary from Motherwell, had been working with young people in Germany for some years and so it transpired that she proposed to bring "one or two young people" from Germany for a few days. At first it all seemed quite manageable. But as time went on, the number of young people coming our way grew on us like Cadbury's roses! Each time Betty made contact with us by phone or by letter, there were more young people joining - and for a longer period of time! When they arrived, I think there were about *sixty* young people, plus their leaders.

Accommodation was a real problem, but when the need arises the Lord seems to provide the answers. Having desperately looked at a variety of options, we were grateful to the local Education Department for offering us Knowetop Special School which was, indeed, far superior to anything that we had even considered. Standing in its own grounds, very quiet, with beds included in the offer, it was a timely and ideal answer to our needs. Thank you Lord!

Betty arranged outings for her young people during the week, and then on a Friday night, there were many, many helpers at that time who came forward to take one, two or three of these young people for the weekend, before bringing them back to the school on a Sunday night. What a tremendous memory, culminating in a special evening in the old Town Hall in Motherwell. This hall held over a thousand people and I remember it being full that night. All of the German young people were on the platform.

The chairman was my good friend Mr T J Smith, a Director of Colvilles Limited. I had invited members of the Town Council and most of them attended. It was really quite an exciting evening, both for the young people from Germany and for our own young people who were involved in helping with the arrangements.

Over the years, the Maranatha Centre invited other visitors and groups from overseas. Principally among them were visits from The Moody Chorale and the Wheaton Male Chorus from the USA. These were glorious occasions when we were able to experience first hand the world class musicianship of friends from America.

THIRTEEN : *A New Home for Maranatha*

We were located in Hope Street for around nine years and I remember, as if it were yesterday, a letter coming from the Council intimating that they required the building as they were going to re-develop the site very shortly. I felt, along with my friends, that, well, it had been good while it lasted but that if the Lord intended that the place should be closed down, so be it! However, about three weeks after the initial letter, the Council invited me to a meeting in the Civic Centre, and it was there that they announced that they would give us a good grant for moving from the premises we were in and that they would help us to find alternative accommodation for another Maranatha Centre.

It was quite unbelievable the way things turned out. We had paid seven hundred and fifty pounds for the building initially and now we were being given a grant for thirteen thousand pounds – just for giving up the old Maranatha Centre! The Council also suggested that we become interested in a building site right behind the new Civic Centre – a prime site, particularly at that time and one that would have cost a lot of money. They offered us that site for four hundred and fifty pounds, so it was really something very, very special.

Excited and inspired, we set to work putting together plans for a new building.

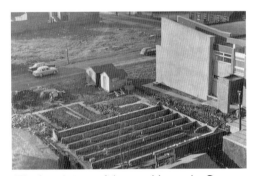

The foundations of the new Maranatha Centre

Dan Ferguson, a member of our Executive Committee, was a builder so he was contracted to do the job.

The building itself, when completed, cost only twenty three thousand pounds and, by the time we turned the key in the door at the opening, the whole of that had been paid with a residue of one hundred and nineteen pounds still in the bank.

As I look back on these amazing events, I praise God for His provision - in the manpower, the finance and the people that the Lord had used to put this building together: a testimony to His faithfulness.

Recollections of the new Centre are inevitably associated with activity and I thank God for so much that went on there. It was there that the Junior Singers were started.

Maranatha Junior Singers

Maranatha Junior Singers

It was there, too, that the Maranatha Camp was born. It continues to this day and has been a great source of blessing to so many.

There was the Radio Team that did a tremendous job of work. This, of course, was the brain child of Alex Lochhead and was staffed by several young people who made the success of programming a priority in their lives, sometimes working until well into the night to complete a programme! Members included Norman Lochhead, Alex Davis, Ian Adams, David Bryson, Richard White, Iain Morris and others.

Originally formed to supply reel to reel tapes to missionaries all over the world, the Radio Team, beginning in the late sixties - and for many subsequent years - established a wide range of outlets for hospital programming. The old Law Hospital near Carluke was the starting point with a production called "Roundabout 4", so called because the time of transmission was 4.15. Patients entering the hospital were given a little bookmark with details and they were able to make requests for hymns and gospel songs. Where possible, those requests were integrated into programmes which developed particular themes.

In addition to Law Hospital, five hospitals were served in the Aberdeen area and two in Kilmarnock. The programme for wider afield had a different name: "These Hymns Have Spoken". The programme was also played in the Sir John Mann home in Bellshill, courtesy of George Little and his father, John.

In every respect, the little studio in the Maranatha Centre was like a professional radio set up except that it had no transmission service. All the tapes were pre-recorded and sent to the location for 'broadcast'. Interested people in other parts of the country took responsibility for the play-out of these programmes on Sunday afternoons or weekday evenings and for negotiating permission with the hospital authorities.

Maranatha Recording Studio

Ian Adams, who became a very successful local businessman, was the youngest of the group. Of quiet demeanour, he was always able to be relied upon when it was necessary to staff the studio well into the night. Ian's concern for the Centre was ongoing throughout his life and that meant a great deal to me. Through his input, today we are able to enjoy a resurgence of interest in the work of the Maranatha Centre. Sadly, Ian died aged forty-seven in 2002.

Most activities in the Centre were scheduled and timetabled for obvious reasons, but there was one which was, as they would express it in today's parlance, "24/7". That was the telephone ministry, "Dial Goodnews". The concept was that callers telephoned a given number in order to hear a short tape recorded message of two minutes duration which was prepared each week by the Maranatha Radio Team. Not only did these messages help and inspire those who called to listen, but, as with so many Christian activities, there was great blessing for those who were involved in organising the communication of the message.

Maranatha Choir

Maranatha Choir

Maranatha Choir

The Maranatha Choir had been established many years before, but it was in the new Centre that the Maranatha Junior Singers came into existence. In many ways, the group epitomised the ministry of the centre: it brought young people together; it encouraged their spiritual development; it gave them purpose; it encouraged the work of evangelism. The young people – there were always around forty in the group – were particularly encouraged in their personal faith relationships, often holding prayer times as part of their rehearsal periods.

Initially started by John Carrick in 1970, the choir leader's baton was passed to Andrew MacLellan. He was followed by Eddie Wilkinson. At all times, the Junior Singers were backed up by a team of administrators and musicians whose input was absolutely indispensable. The Junior Singers travelled all over Scotland and made at least three visits to England. They appeared on one of Scottish Television's religious programmes in the company of storyteller, David Kossoff. Jean Dickson, a team-member involved in taking responsibility for the group confirmed that one of the great benefits for many young people was that it was while they were members of the Junior Singers that they participated in prayer times for the first time in their lives.

Of course, one of the major lasting legacies of the Maranatha Centre was the Maranatha Camp. The aim was to take a large group of young people for a week – traditionally during the first week of what is known locally as Glasgow Fair – for a holiday where the emphasis was two-fold: recreation and spiritual challenge.

Beginning in 1961, the Maranatha Camp has gone right through to the present day without any year being an exception.

Maranatha Camp

Photograph by Perthshire Advertiser

Maranatha Camp

Photograph by Perthshire Advertiser

Its initiation was really quite simple. Alex Lochhead and I called together Sunday School and Bible Class leaders in the area and, out of that group, a committee was formed with rotating chairmanship. The person in charge each year was known as "the commandant". Perhaps some would think the military connotation is significant! Those taking responsibility with their wives, in the early years, included Dan Ferguson, Hugh Miller, Willie Gunn, Jim Wilson, Bert Lamb, Ken Griffiths, Jim Kirkland, Ben Scholfield, Tom Adam and Ken Robb.

The first Maranatha Camp was held in Lochaber High School, Fort William, in 1961 and a return visit was made in 1962. The following year, Cupar Angus was the venue. A special feature of that year was the visit of Betty Rankin with her troupe of young Germans.

In the first three years, the spiritual input – there was a meeting in the morning and a meeting in the evening – was given by Billy Gilmour and Harry Morris. The Camp has been enormously successful and hundreds, if not thousands, of young lives have been influenced for good.

Apart from the meetings themselves, the young people were formed into "houses" and the competitive spirit was bred and developed through week-long sports and other forms of competition. Some of the sporting events were reserved for Wednesdays when parents and friends were invited to pay a visit.

Of course, excursions were organised as well and, in Fort William, there was the inevitable climbing of Ben Nevis. Permit me just one anecdote from that adventure. One young man from Carfin came to us with the disadvantage of having bones that are easily broken. When those who knew him best learned that he intended to join our expedition to the top of Ben Nevis, they warned us to be extra careful with him. Imagine our delight to have accompanied him to the top of "The Ben" and brought him back in complete safety, only to discover that, within ten minutes, he had gone for a shower, slipped and broken his collar bone. You just can't let them out of your sight!

Young people attending the Camps were extremely enthusiastic about their experience and, at the end of the week, many felt emotionally out of sorts as they had to temporarily separate from many friends old and new. Several who attended the Camp in their teens subsequently became leaders and continue to be involved to this day.

The Camp catered for teenagers, but it soon became apparent that there was a 'market' for a different kind of holiday for those whose who had 'outgrown' the Camp. As a result, the Maranatha Centre more or less created its own travel club, arranging holidays for young people to such venues as Norway, Switzerland and, in particular, to Port Stewart in Ireland where, along with evangelist, Hedley Murphy, we used to be involved in an Ulster-Scottish Crusade in the Town Hall. It was really quite tremendous to have anything from eighty to a hundred young people on holiday in these places as well as taking part in evangelistic outreach with Hedley and his brother Jimmy.

I was always enthusiastic about getting as many young people involved as possible in our trips to Ireland and, naturally, would have tried to make the whole experience attractive. John Hunter, who is now an elder in Ebenezer Evangelical Church (formerly Ebenezer Hall), was one of the young people on these holidays and he tells the story of how Wallace had advertised that the houses that we would stay in had a sea view. "Well", he said, "of course we did have a sea view, but I had to stand on a chair and look over a wardrobe before it could be seen". That caused me a wee bit of embarrassment. Maybe I have been known to overstate the case on the odd occasion!

In life, there are so many lessons to be learned and the teaching is done in so many ways. It can even come at unexpected moments - such as the time during a visit to the Carrick-a-Reed Rope Bridge not far from Port Stewart. My good friend, Margaret Inglis, who has not been favoured with sight since her earliest days, was with us on the trip. I was to escort Margaret across this bridge which was very, very shaky, and I could see clearly all the potential dangers as we crossed this great ravine with the water surging through it. It was quite frightening. But Margaret could not see it. Holding tightly to my arm with absolute trust and with no apparent fear, she was able to cross safely to the other side. It is such a picture of how our trust in God can help us remain stable and calm in time of challenge.

Our Port Stewart adventures were never completely over until we arrived home. On one occasion, returning on the coach to Larne, we discovered that the boat we were due to sail on was delayed in coming over from Scotland so there was a large queue of people. What do you do when you are standing around with a crowd of young people other than sing? And, because we had been singing for a fortnight as a choir, we thought it was only natural that we would do so then. Allegedly, I was wearing a soft hat and I remember a man who had consumed quite a lot of alcohol, but who was appreciative of the singing of the young people, took my hat, passed it around the folks who were waiting and came back to present me with a hat full of money - quite an embarrassment but, nevertheless, appreciated by the young people themselves. Later on, one of the girls (I think it might have been Marion Lamb) brought me a cutting from The Sunday Post. A letter had been sent to the paper describing how these Christian young people had been singing and had entertained the folks on the quayside and went on to emphasise how much it had been appreciated by the folks travelling back to Scotland as they waited for the boat to come in.

Over the years, we have been grateful for the productive and high quality relationship that has existed between the Maranatha Centre and the local Council. At the official opening of the new building, Provost Howson, a gracious, quiet and unassuming, man (yes, such qualities do exist among some politicians!) presided over the opening ceremony and officially turned the key in the door.

The new Maranatha Centre

The official ceremony

On many occasions, we have been grateful to receive Civic receptions. Examples are when we welcomed choirs from America. These were often quite lavish affairs and not only presented Motherwell and Scotland in a positive light, but at a practical level, met our needs through providing meals that otherwise we would have had to prepare and serve ourselves.

We were able to follow up such occasions with invitations to the councillors to join us in the concerts that followed and, of course, there they were able to hear an updated account of what was going on at Maranatha, but, in addition, they also heard songs of faith and experienced quality music from groups like The Wheaton Choir, the Moody Chorale and the African Children's Choir. We are so grateful to the civic authorities for their support over so many years and I feel that a particular thanks is due to Provost Hutchie Sneddon who became a long time friend and who was a great encourager of all that we did.

Well appointed though the new Maranatha Centre was, there were many occasions when we needed far larger premises in which to stage high quality Christian events. It was wonderful, therefore, to have the use of the new civic Concert Hall and all its facilities.

I like to consider, however, that perhaps we were able to make a little contribution to giving a high profile to the Civic facilities. In the earliest days, the Council frequently invited entertainers to the Concert Hall but were often unable to fill it. For example, I well remember the Red Army Singers and Dancers – a highly talented and rousing group of performers arriving in Motherwell. The place was perhaps less than half full and that bothered me greatly. I determined at that time that we would do something from Maranatha that would help to put this Civic Concert Hall 'on the map'. And that we did, because about a year later, with the use of the Maranatha Choir, Junior Singers and invited guests, we had an evening of Sacred Song in the Civic Concert Hall. This was so successful that, in subsequent years, we held concerts on four successive nights.

We did foresee that one of those nights would be used ostensibly as a dress rehearsal; but it occurred to me that some of the senior citizens could join us for that and so, over the years on Thursday nights, we would fill the hall with many hundreds of senior citizens who were brought in from all over the district. It was a real joy to have them coming free of charge and this was not only appreciated by the senior citizens themselves, but certainly also by the Council.

Feeding the multitudes

Then sometimes on Friday nights, we would have a dinner – a lavish operation that proved extremely labour-intensive and we were pushed to the limit, but, through doing that, we were certainly able to raise quite a lot of funds for Maranatha. This Friday evening arrangement, however, soon conflicted with the existence of the Council's own caterers. Thereafter, an edict was given that no group was allowed to be self-catering but, instead, would have to use the Council's caterers. That was uneconomic for us but we retained the Friday evening concerts. Saturday concert evenings were always filled to capacity. On Sunday evenings, we held after-church rallies between 8pm and 9.45pm.

These special concerts were also used to continue our interest in encouraging ministers and fulltime workers in the Motherwell district. While we could not any longer give them hospitality on Friday nights in the main Concert Hall, we were able to offer them a meal in a different area of the hall. That was a great source of blessing to us - and to them, I am sure.

An especial highlight within the history of the Civic Concert Hall events was the visit from America of Col James Irwin, scientist, Christian - and astronaut on Apollo 15.

Photograph by Bill Cullen Photography, Newarthill

Jim Irwin meets the Provost of Motherwell

The famous astronaut had an earlier engagement in Dublin to speak of his experiences as an astronaut and a Christian. I was honoured to be telephoned and asked if I would like to have him visit us in Motherwell. I immediately accepted without pondering what interest there would be in such a visit. The date was fixed for Tuesday, 5 September 1978 and the Civic Concert Hall in Motherwell was booked. That was the easy part. The venue would accommodate around twelve hundred people at that time. However, there were not the same very strict regulations controlling the numbers at functions in the Concert Hall as exist today and I reckon that we had close on two thousand people jammed into that venue.

We had arranged for a special PA system to relay the sound to those who could not be seated. It was an inspirational evening and many of those attending were greatly challenged by Jim's testimony as well as being impressed by his exploits in space and the extraordinary preparation that was necessary before he could be selected as an astronaut.

One thing I had not reckoned upon was the immense interest that there would be not only from the Christian public, but from those interested in space travel and, of course, the press. I thank God for His guidance for all that took place.

With such a high profile event, it was important to have just the right chairperson.

As I prayed and rehearsed all the possibilities, I felt directed to William Gillies who lived in Wishaw with his wife and three daughters. Mr Gillies, the managing director of one of the large steelworks, was held in very high esteem.

When I called with the invitation, I was surprised at his response. Laughingly, he asked: "What gave you the idea that I might fit the bill?" To my amazement, he had just returned with his family from some weeks spent in America and, during that time, had visited the NASA space centre and so was relatively clued up about space exploration and readily accepted my invitation.

Jim Irvin's visit made a great impact on many folks, not least of all members of our Town Council, who had granted us a Civic reception and dinner at which Jim spoke briefly. It was encouraging for me to discover that so many of the councillors accepted my invitation to be present at the Concert Hall.

The multi-faceted ministry of the Maranatha has been an inspiration to many hundreds of people over the years and, indeed, the time came when there was so much activity to be co-ordinated and moved forward that the decision was taken to appoint a fulltime worker.

In September 1969, John Carrick was established in the role and, a year later, he was joined by his new wife, Margaret.

John Carrick presented to the Provost of Motherwell

John's inauguration was almost a civic affair with the Provost attending the event and press releases given to the local newspapers.

A unique contribution of John's was the establishment of the Maranatha Junior Singers in the early seventies. We benefited significantly from the input of John and Margaret for around two years, by which time, Jimmy Brown, an Army Scripture Reader for fourteen years, took up post. During his tenure, he was promoted to the Lord's presence. It was a sad moment for us, but a glorious culmination for a life that on earth had been lived for the glory of God. Jimmy was succeeded by Alan Carmichael whose background in social work enabled him to bring an interesting professional perspective to the role. Working alongside his brother-in-law, Sandy Steen, Alan re-focused the ministry of the Centre in conjunction with the social work department of the local Council.

It is inevitable that organisations such as the Maranatha Centre – and indeed churches themselves - go through periods of review and change. This was very much the pattern at Maranatha in these days and no doubt in the future times will arise when there will be questions about the redirection of the work. In all these things we simply pray that the decision makers will continue to be sensitive to God's will and purpose. The Maranatha ministry has achieved much over the last fifty years and it is our prayer that in the future it will go on addressing the spiritual needs of all who are associated with it.

FOURTEEN: *Evangelism In Action*

Ever since 1955, I had been inspired to be involved in the work of evangelism. The All Scotland Crusade had so impacted the nation that it was the hope and prayer of many that the work of evangelism would continue throughout our land.

Carluke Evangelistic Crusade – 7-21 February 1965

My first opportunity to become directly involved in major evangelical activity took place in the mid sixties in South Lanarkshire. Alex Lochhead and I had heard, and read, about Hedley Murphy, an Irish evangelist.

Hedley Murphy, Evangelist

Together, we prayed about the possibility of Hedley's involvement with us and ultimately invited him over to discuss the concept of an evangelistic mission in Scotland. He had not preached here before but had had a lot of success in Ulster. So after prayerful consideration, we decided to invite him back.

The town hall in Carluke was booked for ten days. Alex Lochhead took the responsibility of setting up counselling classes in conjunction with Harry Morris of Glenview Evangelical Church, Gartness, Airdrie. Both had been trained for the Billy Graham Mission in the Kelvin Hall in 1955 and were extremely competent in the necessary skills. The counselling classes were held in Kirkstyle Church in Chapel Street in Carluke. A choir, under the direction of Jim Law, was formed and was a great blessing during the Mission. The practices took place in St Andrew's Parish Church and singers - about seventy of them – were recruited from all over Lanarkshire. The choir pianist was Alistair Lochhead.

It was all very well having counselling classes and choir practices, but it was vitally important to let the people of Carluke know about the Mission. The young man who accepted the responsibility for publicity was David Wilson, a committee member of the Maranatha Centre in Motherwell. A native of Carluke, David knew the town well. He did a fantastic job in organising the many young volunteers necessary for the task in hand. I remember joining them for tea and bacon rolls on three very cold Saturday mornings before encouraging them from God's Word about the great significance of their role. The arrangements made by David were thorough and every home in Carluke was contacted three times. First, there was intimation of the Mission one month before the start-up along with an invitation to attend it. A second invitation went out one week before the Mission and a third was issued one day before its commencement. It was thrilling to experience the enthusiasm of those young people. A good number were from the various churches in Carluke and, of course, from further afield.

The Rev Brian Kingsmore, another Ulsterman and minister of the Congregational Church in Airdrie, was invited to chair all of the meetings. He had a very pleasant disposition and was very wise in his conduct of the services. What a thrill it was, night after night, to see the four hundred adults at the main service being preceded by three hundred children at their own special meeting at which Alison Davidson and Robin Lochhead provided accompaniment on the piano and organ respectively. At the adult meetings, the town hall was more or less filled to capacity.

Hedley was a gifted preacher who was able to hold the attention of children as well as adults. The ministry of the choir was greatly appreciated and, indeed, it became known as the Maranatha Choir and continued for over thirty years.

David Wilson and his band of young people had established what had been intended, that of making the people of Carluke aware of the Mission. All of us involved were, of course, greatly encouraged as, each evening, young people and older people responded to the challenge of the gospel preaching by Hedley Murphy. Those who were counselled - and there were many who professed faith in the Lord Jesus Christ - were encouraged to go back to their churches where follow up arrangements had been made for their spiritual wellbeing.

One interesting anecdote from my ongoing relationship with Hedley Murphy was the interest he showed in, would you believe, the registration number of my car. At the time, my white Austin Maxi had the number HGM 999E. Hedley's eyes lit up at the prospect of acquiring it. Think of it! A man with the initials HGM and the mission of an evangelist. Eventually, he acquired the number and the interpretation was that Hedley G Murphy, Evangelist, with a 999 hotline to heaven!

Jesus Alive '75

Ten years later and the story of involvement with missions continued with *Jesus Alive '75* at which the preacher was the Rev George B Duncan of the Tron Church in Glasgow.

Rev George B Duncan

As is evident from the Mission title, the year was 1975, but for up to three years previously, prayer meetings had been held in the Maranatha Centre. It had always been my conviction that if we were going to reach the people in our neighbourhood, it had to be achieved through the various churches working together. To that end, for some time, we had a group of committed men and women praying together. Among them were the Rev William Bruce from

Dalziel Parish Church, the Rev Eddie Weir from St Margaret's Parish Church, Pastor Hugh Clark of the King's Church, the Rev Douglas Ross of Motherwell Baptist Church and the Methodist minister - an elderly man who taught me many things. Also regularly joining us was Noel McCullins from Wishaw Baptist Church and many other key lay people, all of whom attended regularly each Saturday at 8 am. Indeed, so much importance did these ministers attach to their role as prayer warriors that, even when they had to conduct a funeral service later on a Saturday morning, they would typically arrange to be picked up by the funeral car at the Centre and taken directly to the church. So committed were they to our times of prayer.

If the seeds of the Mission were rooted in the prayer meetings, the dynamics of how it began to come together were concentrated in just one morning, when it was proposed by one of our members that we should have a joint mission. It appeared quite extraordinary to us to learn that most of us in the room had been pondering the same possibility and we were all similarly motivated. Excitement rose so much that we decided to re-convene in the middle of that week to move plans forward instead of leaving our next discussion until the following weekend.

I recall that mid week meeting very distinctly: spending time in prayer before going on to determine when the Mission should take place, how it should take place, who should be involved and who would come to preach. That was a very special meeting.

Several names were suggested but the person who headed the list was the Rev George B Duncan. Mr Duncan would never have considered himself primarily an evangelist but everyone who knew him would agree that he could powerfully preach the gospel and bring the challenge of God's Word to audiences. I was given the task of contacting him and was quite surprised when he was positive enough to ask for time to consider the proposal. What a joy it was to hear from him just within a week, or thereabouts, that he had agreed to come.

Jesus Alive '75

Photographs by Bill Cullen Photography, Newarthill

Motherwell's Civic Concert Hall was booked for eight days. Various people were appointed to key jobs and so we got on with setting up the Mission. Jimmy Brown, a very good friend of mine and a well known church organist, accepted the responsibility of leading a two hundred voice choir. Rev Willie Bruce accepted the chairmanship of the Mission; Eddie Weir took on the task of putting together a counselling team and so it went on. It was wonderful to see things coming together. It was truly a heart-warming experience for me to see something similar to our Mission in Carluke, held around ten years earlier, where churches had worked together to touch their area and became a great blessing to so many.

In *Jesus Alive '75*, many people professed faith in the Lord Jesus Christ; many more were impacted by the gospel, preached so faithfully each evening by Mr Duncan.

One lasting impact on me was the humility of the preacher. He was used to preaching to many thousands at Keswick and other Christian conventions around the world, yet every morning he called my office to ascertain what I had thought about the Mission so far. Typically he would ask, "Did I preach too long?" To think of a man of his spiritual standing asking a mere mortal like myself such a question! Perhaps that humility played a key part in bringing so much blessing to his life.

Each evening on the programme, we had special guests: singers and people to give testimony. One guest, David McNee, who was at that time the Chief Constable for Strathclyde, came to sing and gave testimony.

Many blessings flowed from his contribution, particularly to other leading members of the police force whom I know were present at that time.

Afterwards, we invited David McNee for supper and it was as if our home had become the headquarters of Strathclyde Police Authority because along with one of his assistants, Ian Alexander, he spent quite a considerable time on the telephone checking up on the post-match events of an important football fixture that had taken place that day. There had been a bit of crowd trouble and he wanted to be certain that matters were under control.

On the final evening of the Mission, we looked back with gratitude and emotion on a monumental event that I am sure brought glory to God. After the counselling had been given and most of the crowds had departed, all those of us who had been involved in our prayer group, and who had been working in the Mission, spent a very special hour in a communion service conducted by the Rev Eddie Weir. That was a truly memorable time of thanksgiving and the recollection of it stirs me to this day.

Later on that year, I was given the honour of being nominated for (and I accepted) the Citizen of the Year Award for our Motherwell District.

Citizen of the Year   Photograph by County Newsphotos, Motherwell

Some years after that, when I was looking at the press photograph from that time, and all that had been written about the event, reality dawned: it was for my *services to evangelism* that this award had been given. It was with a mixture of humility and pride that I realised that someone could be honoured in this world for helping to proclaim the gospel of Jesus Christ. It is so encouraging to think that civic authorities would consider evangelism so significant but it is even more exhilarating to know that, when we humbly work for the glory of God, He plans to reward our service in eternity.

Luis Palau Mission, Strathclyde Country Park, May 1980

After *Jesus Alive '75*, the prayer group continued and, in 1978, we invited Luis Palau to come to preach in Motherwell. The event which was convened would allow us to assess, under God's guidance, the appropriateness of extending an invitation to this international evangelist to join with us in special missions activity at a future date.

The service took place in Crosshill Parish Church where the minister was the Rev Stuart Dunn. A large number attended and those of us who had been involved in giving the invitation were sufficiently encouraged to invite Luis Palau back to head up a major evangelical outreach in the area.

Ian Leitch, a Scottish Evangelist and a very good friend of mine, was very helpful at this time of preparation. He was well acquainted with Luis Palau and that relationship proved invaluable.

We rented an office in the old town hall in Motherwell and that became our missions headquarters. As for the Mission itself, we decided it would be held in a tent! But where to find one? The Rev George Duncan was associated with the Keswick Convention ministry and, of course, their meetings are held in large tents and, as a first option, we looked at the possibility of using the Keswick tent. However, this proved to be impracticable and the next move, again suggested by Mr Duncan, was to make contact with a group in Ireland who had been using a large tent for mission purposes. In turn, I discovered that this tent was owned by people in Leicester, England. I wrote to them, framing my letter in such a way that we suggested we would hire the tent from them. Imagine my reaction when I was told: "Wallace, we are not in the tent hiring business; we're in the soul saving business. If you are in the same business as we are, you can have the tent".

Under discussion was a large circus-style tent, seating around three thousand people. This was the beginning of something quite unbelievable because these dear people not only supplied the tent, but they arranged its transport to Motherwell, too. This required two forty foot trailers. They also provided us with someone who would oversee the erection of the tent and its removal at the conclusion of our planned event. All we were required to do was to have forty men on the site when the tent arrived so that the lorries could be successfully unloaded and returned to base. It was unbelievable to see how quickly such a large tent was erected and it looked very good. We also had to arrange for three thousand seats and this was also achieved in a very wonderful way. The platform area came as part of the tent, so that was extremely helpful. Another staging requirement was for the accommodation of a large choir.

As before, the Rev William Bruce of Dalziel Parish Church, was chairman of the committee and chaired the Mission meetings as well. The Rev Eddie Weir from St Margaret's Parish Church again took the responsibility for arranging the pre-mission counselling classes and the counselling at the tent meetings.

Being responsible for a large tent temporarily set up in the middle of a public park brought special challenges. One of these was the requirement to have security on the site since such a large tent would be vulnerable to vandalism. In order that we could have on-site security around the clock, we were able to procure three fine caravans which were gifted to us for the duration of the Mission by the company

G F Sharp, Builders from Wishaw. I had known the directors of this company and knew that they had used caravans to decant people while they were modernising their homes. They arranged delivery of the caravans onto the site and their collection after the Mission.

So far, arrangements were going well. However, I still needed to consider security personnel very carefully. I believe the Lord prompted me to recall that a friend of mine, Bob McKillop, was a retired Police Inspector. I felt he might just be the man to take the responsibility of arranging security. I well remember one morning in my office determining to telephone Bob at his place of work. His comment to me was that he was just about to have his morning break and could he come down and see me so that we could discuss the situation. He duly arrived and it was quite unbelievable that he, that morning, had been praying - knowing the Mission was taking place - and had been wondering how he might contribute. We talked together and I outlined what I thought would be necessary. Bob accepted responsibility and did a fantastic job, also arranging for volunteers to be there around the clock looking after everything that was on site.

So far, so good; everything seemed to be coming together. I had the bright idea that because we were using the Strathclyde Country Park that Strathclyde Regional Council would require to give their permission. More than that, I felt that maybe the Council would be pleased about what we were doing and give us a bit of encouragement. They had large offices in Hamilton and I felt that we should maybe ask them if it would be possible for us to have a Civic reception as this would help raise the profile of the Mission. I determined to telephone and ask their head office in Glasgow if they would perhaps do something along these lines. The person I spoke to on the telephone listened to all that I had to say and at the end of the conversation he said to me, "Well, Wallace, what is it you want me to do?" I had not even mentioned my name, but this person, Alistair McGibbon, who had a very important and key role to play within Strathclyde Region, clearly recognised my voice. Infamy has its advantages.

Alistair took in hand to arrange a reception in the Banqueting Hall in Hamilton. Luis was able to speak to the gathered company which included all of the Council members and their wives: quite an array of important people and this event, of course, received a lot of publicity in our local newspapers. We were very happy to have that significant advertising. Incidentally, Alistair McGibbon became a great friend of mine and over many years we have met and prayed together and he is one of our trustees now at Maranatha.

And so the Mission itself got underway. Night after night, Luis Palau preached the gospel. The tent was usually filled to capacity. Many people professed faith in Jesus Christ and were counselled at that time. They were encouraged to return to their own churches where they would be looked after spiritually.

The weather during that time was very favourable indeed and there was so much to appreciate, including the way so many volunteers came forward and, as a team, did an excellent job.

As I move around, even after all these years, I meet people whose lives were changed during these days.

One nightmare scenario that occurred half way through the Mission was that one evening I had a telephone call from our friends in Leicester, owners of the tent, to say that they would not be able to uplift the tent as arranged and, instead, we needed to have it taken to the next location which was in Hull, Yorkshire.

Initially, this caused quite a bit of distress but, again, the Lord put into my heart the person I should call. Haulage contractors, James and Alex Smith from Madiston, near Falkirk, were friends of mine. I determined to telephone them to see if they could help - only to be told by Alex Smith that they had sold the business to a multi-national company. However, he was very kind and gave me the name of a person I could telephone who was based in their depot at London Road in Glasgow.

This I did and it was quite unbelievable that they were able to supply me with two forty foot trucks with trailers to come at the appointed time. We had the necessary forty brave men there to help with the dismantling and loading of the tent on to the transport. However, cue the next challenge: the tent had not to be delivered to Hull for another ten days and I had to ask these good people in Glasgow if they could keep the trucks in storage for us for ten days before they delivered to Hull!

Looking back, it just seems like a dream that all these things came together and that the tent was successfully delivered to Hull on the due date. The folks who owned the tent had suggested that they did not wish to have any payment but we felt strongly that we should make a fairly substantial gift to them on account of their incredible generosity.

A residual problem was that I did not know how much we would be charged for transport costs to Hull and, for many weeks after the Mission, I kept concerning myself as to whether we were going to get a very large bill. However, this anxiety was put to rest about six weeks later when, one evening, I received a telephone call from Alex Smith.

When my wife Nettie told me that Alex was on the telephone I had visions of a large bill about to come my way or, perhaps, even worse, the account having been sent out and not received. However, the Lord was still in control. Instead of telephoning to discuss finance, Alex was contacting me to invite me to sing at the opening of an extension to their church! I remember saying, "Alex, in the light of all your kindness to me, I will come to Madiston to sing even if I have to walk there!" "Wallace, there is no problem", he replied, "I have been only too glad that I have been able to help you". So another reason to praise the Lord.

FIFTEEN: *Difficult Choices*

In the early sixties, on the domestic front, an opportunity arose to do what I considered to be a good piece of business: to sell the house in Manse Road in Motherwell and to buy a much larger property at 49 Kitchener Street, Wishaw for the same price as we received for the Manse Road property.

Together in Kitchener Street

By now, the children were attending school in Wishaw – Barbara at Wishaw High School and the boys at Wishaw Public School. Barbara was very interested in sports and was particularly involved in hockey and athletics. Ultimately she became the school captain. That was an honour that I did not fully appreciate at the time.

At the Public School, the boys were experiencing difficulty because they had neither interest in, nor aspiration for, academic matters. Nettie tried hard by helping them with their work.

Our accommodation in Wishaw stood in its own grounds and that proved to be both an advantage and a disadvantage. On one occasion, returning from holiday, we discovered we had been burgled. Indeed, that was not to be the only time. This contributed in a major way to a sense of unease that we had about that house.

Although there were, indeed, many happy memories, another source of sadness is in connection with our boxer pet called Bruce. We had acquired him through friends in the church, Mr & Mrs Andrew Steen, who used to 'show' and breed boxer dogs. We had Bruce from a young age. He proved to be quite a challenge sometimes.

I remember returning home with Nettie one evening and, having locked Bruce in the kitchen beforehand, we were dismayed to discover that, during our absence, he had totally destroyed two legs of the kitchen table. That table had been continuously in use and so we were very inconvenienced!

But just as we were having a difficult time with Bruce, he himself was also living with stress. He had been injured through contact with a car, we think, and his hind quarters had been hurt. He became rather carnaptious as a result of which he had to be muzzled. Eventually, I had the task of taking Bruce to the veterinary college near Anniesland Cross in Glasgow and their conclusion was that Bruce should be put down. I arrived back with his lead and muzzle but without Bruce. Every time his name was mentioned, for some time thereafter, there was weeping. It was like a major death in the family. It was terrible and I declared there would be no more dogs. But there were far more important choices afoot.

The Maranatha Centre – in its new premises – was, by now, becoming a major focus for my attention. In my heart, my main interests were fixed on Christian activity, much more than the economics of business practice. Thereafter began a radical re-think about the place of business in my life and I went through a process of seriously reviewing my priorities.

At this stage, business life was on two levels: the wholesale fruit and potato merchants and the retail shops in Wishaw, Motherwell and Bellshill. Most 'text books' on business life will tell you that a business is either growing or shrinking; it never stands still. To grow a business usually involves an increasing investment of time and finance, sometimes reaching the point where it is the all-consuming focus of one's life. As I considered the significance of dedication to God's service, I realised the business development route was not my priority.

In connection with my spiritual interest, I have an indebtedness to Doris Wright, whom Nettie and I had known for quite some time. From her home in Witney, she used to send us tapes of Bible teaching and I listened to them regularly in the early morning. There have been times in my life when I have encountered men and women of God and longed to know the secret of their happiness and strength. The tapes I was listening to at that time were a great inspiration and led to a deepening of my understanding and commitment.

In Ebenezer, I had a Bible Class with about sixty to seventy young people. I was not well qualified to be a Bible teacher, but there were others in the church who had the necessary experience and skills. For my part, I took on the job of developing and 'marketing' the Bible Class. I set up six separate classes: junior boys and junior girls, intermediate boys and intermediate girls and senior boys and senior girls.

Marketing of the Bible Class included making it attractive and varied for its members. Others who helped me with the work, and whose input I so much appreciated, were Bert and Mary Lightbody, Ian Beckwith, George Hunter, Jenny Lanyon, Jack Watt and Marion Lamb. These were great people and did a very, very good job.

My Bible Class commitment, as well as my involvement in Maranatha, caused me to reach a crisis in my life and to realise that there were important choices ahead and I would need to make them most carefully. My real passion was to be involved in Christian activity. An important decision was taken to reduce the size of our business.

So, first I put the Wishaw shop on the market and, after a month or two, one of the largest retailers in Scotland, Malcolm Campbell, showed an interest in acquiring the shop. It was difficult to know what purchase price we could expect for this business that we had built up.

I recall asking my brother Jim, and another friend Joe Wilson, what the value of the property and the business might be and, having listened to them, I determined to put a challenge to the Lord: I would make it difficult for the prospective buyer and, if it was the Lord's will for this transaction to go through, then the obstacle I had placed there would not prevent the outcome that was according to His will. In fact, I doubled the price that Jim and Joe had suggested!

After a few months of wrangling to and fro, the deal was sealed in my home in Kitchener Street. The buyers had come to meet with me and had offered a price that was within five hundred pounds of the amount that I had set. I knew by then it was right to sell the business! The shops at Bellshill and Motherwell were also subsequently sold – the latter to Archie and Betty Simpson, my brother and sister-in-law.

Crucially, at this point, Nettie and I covenanted with God to commit our lives more fully to Him. We envisaged the likelihood that we were embarking on a journey that would take us, more or less, into fulltime Christian service. I recall this being a time of peace in our lives – and, significantly, a time when we felt God was working out His purpose in us.

Nevertheless, there was also the temptation to become very self-satisfied with what 'I had done'. As with many others in business, I had a mortgage, the car was on hire purchase - as were the lorries. Now with the income from Malcolm Campbell it was the first time in my experience that I owned a house and I also owned the car. I was very happy. However, I had covenanted with God to work as near to full time as possible in my Christian activities. The work at Maranatha was growing and I was anxious to see more and more being done in the work of evangelism and reaching people for Jesus Christ. I still continued to rise early and read and pray and, for quite some time - a year, or perhaps two - I really felt strong and encouraged in the Lord. I felt I had done the right things. God prospered the work of Maranatha at that time and various other activities in which I was engaged. Meanwhile, there was the question of what to do with the wholesale business that we had retained.

My family was growing up – the two boys were at secondary school by now and I knew that they were never going to be architects or lawyers or doctors and that we would need to think about their future work prospects. As a result, we established our wholesale business at Knowetop in Motherwell. This had the obvious advantage of giving employment to Archie and Jimmy, as well as my new son-in-law, Alan Law. As I look back on my life now I realise I put the boys before the Lord and I re-energised the business so that they could be well established in work.

Of course, me being me, I had to be involved as well and that began to take up my time. Around then, I benefited from the support and help of a younger friend who had worked with me in the Bible Class for many years - Jack Watt. Business progressed but, looking back, I realise that this was the slippery slope – even though everything seemed to be fine. Slowly but surely, business began to take over my life again. On reflection, I am sure I should never have been in business. I never had enough discipline and would always have been better working under authority. The real issue was not so much a weakness in me but, more, that my heart lay in working with young people and in the church. And if I was involved in anything, I gave it one hundred per cent. It was difficult to do that in two spheres of operation.

The working days continued to be long and the amount of effort and organisation required by the wholesale business was very considerable. Meanwhile, another business – that of a close friend, Robert Anderson, who had recently died - was being put up for sale. His line had been the supply and installation of fireplaces. In conjunction with my brothers Jim and George, we took the opportunity to re-focus our business interests and, in time, we bought Anderson's Fireplaces.

By now, working life, church life and our Maranatha activities were all Motherwell based and we decided that, all things considered, we should move back to Motherwell. We purchased a newly built house at 18 Muirhead Terrace and named it 'Maranatha'. The name was produced in wrought iron by a skilled colleague of mine at the Centre - David Wilson, a blacksmith by profession. We were happy in that home and the name of the house somehow symbolised a real sense of belonging.

Happy in Muirhead Terrace

Under its new owners, Andersons Fireplaces at first seemed to prosper and grow to the point where we moved from our quite small premises at Knowetop to a large showroom in Brandon Street, Motherwell. With that new acquisition came new financial responsibilities but we felt these business decisions would be helpful in securing the employment future of the boys.

Looking back, I believe I can clearly conclude that not only was this a step too far, but that we had moved well away from what we had covenanted to do. For a variety of reasons, we decided that our future no longer lay in business and we decided to close it down.

Friends Walter and Sharon Watson

I telephoned my friend Walter Watson in Ireland knowing of his interest in anything that Nettie and I were engaged in. I did not reckon on his reaction. He asked me to arrange a meeting with my bank manager and my accountant - both Christians (Bob MacGillivray and Alan McGregor). When I had indicated to them earlier the route out of business that I had proposed to take (ie, selling all my assets including the house and cars), their reaction was quite amazing. They said, "Wallace, we have never heard of anyone acting quite like this". They had in mind that, in these circumstances, most people would try to protect their home and salvage as much as possible for themselves. On a previous occasion, my advice had been canvassed by a man who was also closing down his business. I remember advising him that "if your name is above the door, your name is also associated with the business and if people know that you are a Christian, the only real course of action open to you is to do everything you can to meet your creditors". It was time for me to take my own advice. In any case, I did not believe I had any other option. I was well known as a Christian in the town and I had to honour the Lord and my own testimony and that of the church. Within forty-eight hours, a meeting was arranged with the bank manager, the accountant and Walter from Ireland.

As the professionals outlined the financial situation, perhaps hoping to dissuade Walter from getting involved, he turned to them and said, "He is my friend and I will take care of any shortfall". I can hear his comment even to this day. It is as fresh in my memory now as it was real all those years ago. This ended the business venture that I should never have had in the first place, having gone back on covenanting with the Lord that I would work full time in His service.

You soon learn that you can never break a covenant that was made with God. Neither should we break covenants made with other people. This was a lesson that I had to learn.

Herewith started my life of real spiritual learning: to lean on the One who has become more precious as the days, weeks and years have passed. What had gone before was a humbling experience and I thank God that, in the midst of all the trauma of letting the business go, I was cast solely on Him. The lesson that I had to learn was that if I did not humble myself, He would humble me big time - and He surely did that. Even as I write, the following verse of a hymn comes to mind:

> All the way my Saviour leads me;
> What have I to ask beside?
> Can I doubt His tender mercies,
> Who through life has been my guide?

I thank God for that sentiment that I can truly underscore.

And so in faith we relied upon God to lead us as we closed the door on 18 Muirhead Terrace – a home that we loved - and made our way into an unknown future.

At the close of this chapter, it is highly appropriate to conclude with a word about Nettie. She proved so faithful and worked so hard throughout all of our business life. She also had to give up our lovely home and car as we moved out. Never once did she look back and say, "I wish this had not happened" and I know she knew, as I did, that I went back on my promise to the Lord.

Failure with God is never final, nor does God abandon us in our time of need. Just around then, in His perfect timing, a property at Biggar became available and colleagues in the Maranatha Centre felt that this would be a great place to establish a Christian holiday and conference centre. Nettie and I were invited to become involved in setting it up, thus giving us accommodation away from Motherwell and also away from the stresses of the business break up. In Biggar, we would have space to get our lives back together again. Living around twenty-five miles from Motherwell, it was not practicable for me to maintain my involvement with the Maranatha Centre in Motherwell and so retired from active service there. Nevertheless, I was enthusiastic about the new challenge that Maranatha Biggar would present.

SIXTEEN : A 'Biggar' Maranatha

The Maranatha Conference Centre at Biggar was an exciting concept. Whereas the Maranatha Centre is in the middle of an industrial town and reasonably close to the homes of the majority of those who attended it, Biggar offered much more in the way of a developed leisure experience and was, of course, designed to be residential. Set in the rolling countryside of South Lanarkshire, the little market town has idyllic qualities by contrast with Motherwell, which fairly bustles with working life.

The peace and tranquillity in Biggar made an immediate impact. However, the condition of the facility we were considering did not quite harmonise with the beauty of the agricultural environment in which it was located.

The economics of the leasing could not have been more favourable. Thanks are due to Alan Carmichael who negotiated the lease - it spanned twenty years from its starting point in 1986. The Centre was owned by South Lanarkshire Council and was leased to Maranatha at a peppercorn rent of five pounds per annum. The original purpose of the building had been to accommodate asthmatic patients but had only been used for two and half years. It had been left unoccupied for some time and had been vandalised. I first visited the place with Alex Lochhead - and what a shock it was. There were no windows on the ground floor, the roof was leaking substantially and the parquet flooring was floating around by now in a foot of water. The boiler that heated the whole building was defunct and there were hundreds of burst pipes. Maybe that puts the lowly rent in another perspective!

How this place was made habitable in such a short time was nothing short of miraculous. The small flat on the first floor was allocated to Nettie and me and we were able to move in after it had been made watertight - nearly. The poor condition of the rest of the building meant that we had to barricade ourselves in - closing the stairwell leading to the first floor to give us a sense of safety. This arrangement was needed for about a month until the rest of the building was secured. The number of people involved in getting the building ready for business was quite incredible. How God brought skilled engineers like Louis Howson and Robert Jackson! The skills and ingenuity of these men got the boiler operating and what a blessing that was. Louis had an important job as chief engineer of some of the major hospitals in Lanarkshire; Robert Jackson worked on the oil rigs, spending twelve weeks offshore followed by twelve weeks at home.

I saw my job only as the 'go-for' - running the errands, making the tea, anything that kept those important people working.

I remember one day coming down John's Loan, the road leading from the town centre to the new Maranatha Conference Centre. I was bringing supplies for the troops, when, all of a sudden, I saw a cloud of black smoke coming from the boilerhouse chimney. I am not sure if anyone heard me, but I cried out "Praise the Lord!". It was such a wonderful indication of progress. Later that day, we found out that there was nearly a full tank of fuel. This had lain there for two and half years and turned out to be sufficient to enable us to dry out the whole of the building.

Words will always be inadequate to praise sufficiently the workers who succeeded in getting our Biggar Conference Centre operative. The reinstatement of the parquet flooring was a laborious job but was done in a very short time by volunteers. A very fine young man, John Stevenson, had a specialist 'suspended ceilings' business. As a result, we were able to have suspended ceilings throughout the building.

It was wonderful to see so many people work tirelessly to put in place the wind and waterproof ceilings that we needed and in such a short time span. I knew John Stevenson to be a very fine Christian and it was no surprise when, later, he transferred his business interests to his family and thereafter became a Church of Scotland minister.

New ceilings led to new wall coverings. Andy Sharp was a recovering alcoholic who was a painter and decorator to trade and he applied his skills to the renovation of the small lounge on the ground floor at Maranatha. He stripped the walls and prepared everything before hanging his anaglypta paper. It looked really good, but the problem was that in the morning when we came downstairs, all the paper had detached itself from the wall and was drooping towards the floor! Andy was quite disconsolate. However, he was able to remedy the situation and that room remains, I think, to this day with that same paper.

Mentioning specific names is hazardous given that I have such a faltering memory. There were just so many people involved and each of them needs to know how grateful we are for all that was achieved. I am so glad that, by contrast, God does not forget and I know that our helpers, all of them - the ones mentioned and the ones not mentioned - will get their reward.

The Opening of the Biggar Maranatha Centre

Photograph by Carluke & Lanark Gazette

And so a date was set for the opening. I must mention that, before the day came, a group of twelve ladies - headed by my great friend Sadie Weir from Benhar Evangelical Church – volunteered to come over and, armed with buckets, scrubbing brushes and cleaning gear, did a great job in making the place look its best for that open day.

Just prior to the event itself, I had a visit from a special friend, McKie Munn who brought with him a fine, new brown suit – just my size! "The manager needs to look his best for the visitors," he quipped. McKie and Gladys Munn, who lived in Lanark, were truly God-sent during these days and helped Nettie and me many times over the ensuing years. The work at the centre was to be hard and demanding and how wonderful to escape, at times, to the home of McKie and Gladys and enjoy their friendship and be encouraged spiritually.

The first open event was on a Saturday when all our Maranatha friends on the mailing list were invited to come and see for themselves what was going on. We were also delighted to welcome a host of dignitaries, including local councillors and the minister of Biggar Church of Scotland, the Rev Cameron McKenzie. I well remember that, on the day, about half an hour before the first of our friends began to arrive, there was delivery of ten three piece suites that had been ordered for the large lounge area, and I recall lifting them in with some help and taking the plastic sheeting from them. Even as we put them in place in the lounge, the friends started arriving and that furniture was in use from the very first moment! It was a great feat of timing by the delivery people and we thank God for that.

During the event itself we benefited greatly from the help of another group of ladies, arranged by Liz Howson, from the Forth Mission Church. They came to provide the visitors with tea and coffee and home baking and what a great job they did. The aroma of freshly baked scones and pancakes from the kitchen filled the dining room where our friends settled down after their tour of the building. On that day, over 200 visitors came and expressed their surprise and delight at what had been accomplished.

Many of my colleagues at Marantha would be surprised if I did not mention the use of offering boxes on the day. These were very large free will containers with the words *Free Will Offering* engraved on the front; more often they were called 'Wallace's friends'. They were always put within reach of those wishing to help us financially. It also helped to 'jar' their memory if they had forgotten to think about the financing of this project.

Cartoon courtesy of Allan Stevenson

During the Biggar years, I was deeply impressed by how Maranatha drew so many unsolicited offers of help. Such volunteering was touching and greatly appreciated.

I remember on one very cold and snowy morning, there were no guests in the Maranatha Centre and the front door had been locked. The bell rang and, upon answering it, I found a diminutive young lady who introduced herself as Kathleen Rodgers. She intimated that she was a Christian and that she had been helping for quite a few years with Scripture Union and wondered if she could be of any help to us. I was really encouraged by Kathleen's visit and she came and helped us on quite a number of occasions. She has been a friend for a number of years now and still attends the Church of Scotland in Biggar.

And so the work of Maranatha at Biggar got well underway, providing highly satisfactory facilities for groups of all shapes and sizes to come for relaxation, fellowship and spiritual refreshment. I have many cherished memories of hundreds of contacts made and friendships established.

Helen Wilson, one of our guests, so appreciated the Biggar experience that she expressed her thoughts in verse, as follows:

REFLECTIONS ON A VISIT HERE!

Come inside and rest awhile
"Be Still", and wait upon THE LORD
Pause from your work, your daily toil
And listen quietly to HIS WORD
When hearts are bruised and spirits low
"Come Unto Him" – and be refreshed.
Your troubled heart He'll set aglow
For each of us, He knows what's best.
His loving arms are ever near
Outstretched to gather us within
His back is bent to pick us up
When we His children stoop to sin.
Within these walls His servants are
Ready to speak the living Word
To minister to all our needs
With love, to praise the living Lord
May you experience like me, my friend
Refreshment, rest, new faith, when here your stay is o'er
That when you leave this place, your visit at an end
Your prayer will be, one day you will return for more.

Arriving for the Biggar Experience!

One thing that impressed me was the sheer variety of groups that came our way, though sometimes the juxtaposition of certain arrivals and departures led to a wry smile. For example, there was the occasion when we had a group of ladies from the Church of God in Lanarkshire. They belonged to a rather exclusive type of Brethren fellowship. By early Sunday evening, it was time for them to leave. At that same time, I had arranged to meet with another group who had come to view the Centre: members of the Evangelical Sisters of Mary. While the ladies from the Church of God were loading their cars, the new group arrived in religious dress. Here we were with one group of highly conservative Brethren ladies in a direct encounter with a number of ladies dressed in habits that one associates more obviously with the Catholic faith. Their base was in Germany and, indeed, they spent time with us on more than one occasion.

We had many different groups and it was a great experience for me to have my horizons widened as I met so many people who came for midweek breaks and shared their experiences of being involved in a wide variety of ministries - including ministry to the Jews. I often reflected that, at Biggar, we catered for everybody: the charismatics, the asthmatics and even the rheumatics!

Being a residential centre with its own dining facilities, Biggar offered us obvious opportunities to convene special dinners. These were held once a month with a view to helping raise funds for - and create awareness of - the Centre among many of the folks living in the towns around Lanarkshire and elsewhere. The dinners were always very well attended. We had speakers and singers of real quality. And so we had the recipe for real success: enjoyable food, splendid fellowship, spiritual challenge and much needed fund-raising.

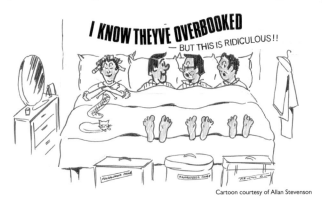

Cartoon courtesy of Allan Stevenson

However, the highlight of our year at Biggar was surely the annual visit of the children from Humbie. The children were accompanied by their carers, including Rosa, Jean and Betty and Mima Waugh. These were the ladies who had that amazing vision for looking after those lovely down's syndrome children. We were privileged to give them hospitality for a week each year. Later, we would visit them in Humbie and it was great to meet up with them there. The love and affection given to these young people by their carers is riveted in my memory.

Although most people came in groups, some came as individuals. One single Mum who came to us from Motherwell received much needed care, relaxation and even some counselling. She had a baby and I always remember that, to give her a bit of peace, I used to take the baby for a walk. I used to encourage the baby to walk for herself and, indeed, she took her first steps at Biggar. It never occurred to me that such a simple act would impact the mother so much but I have since met her on several occasions and, on each one, she has recalled that her baby took her first steps at Maranatha in Biggar. Somehow that symbolised for me what we were trying to achieve there: that many people would take their first steps to a life with Jesus Christ through the witness of the Centre there at Biggar.

With so many Christian groups coming and going, there were plenty of opportunities to have warm and rich Christian fellowship on a regular basis. We were also able to arrange our own fellowship with local people and that proved to be very interesting.

On a Tuesday evening, when there were rarely guests at the Centre, we would convene a Bible study. Attending were folks like Harry and Jean Parker from Symington, Robert and Elizabeth Jackson from Biggar, Billy and Jenny Davidson from Biggar, along with others helping in the Centre at that particular time. Sometimes we had the opportunity to meet with missionaries, or other special visitors, on these Tuesday evenings and there was a real sense of fellowship on these occasions. At this point, I would like to pay special tribute to the tireless effort expended by Billy and Jenny Davidson in connection with the Centre. We will never know just how much of their time was consumed by the responsibilities they took on at Biggar and their help was absolutely indispensable.

As well as enjoying our fellowship evenings, it was important for us to be associated with a local place of worship and Nettie and I attended the local Church of Scotland where we benefited from the ministry of the Rev Cameron McKenzie, formerly of St Mary's Parish Church in Motherwell. I really enjoyed these services because they were encouraging and uplifting – not least of all because the church was full every Sunday morning and the congregation included a sizeable number of young people. Rev McKenzie was always eloquent and sincere as he addressed the young people and I was particularly impressed also with the lessons he applied to the children. His wife and he visited us on some occasions and we were also invited to the manse. We became firm friends during that time but, sadly, some time later, Cameron and his wife were both involved in a serious car accident on the road between Biggar and Edinburgh and soon afterwards, Cameron McKenzie retired from the parish church in Biggar.

Although the Centre was primarily set up for the benefit of those who would travel to the area, we also wanted to impact the local community as much as possible. One important connection was with the local high school and involved David Geddes, the Scripture Union worker for the whole of Lanarkshire. Along with David, we met the Headteacher at Biggar High School and this led to David coming on other occasions. The SU group that was formed developed quite steadily thereafter.

Sadly, David's wife, Alice, died suddenly and prematurely, but I've always appreciated and admired how David handled that situation. He is still enthusiastic about spiritual work, particularly that of evangelism. David and I continue to meet once a month with other ministers and church leaders for a time of prayer. I always find this very encouraging and challenging.

Despite being in Biggar to serve others, there were opportunities for us to discover the area around the town for ourselves. I recall with particular pleasure the walks we took and sometimes the drives right over the hill behind Biggar to Broughton before wending our way to Tweedsmuir and then continuing over the hills to the Megit dam. It was wonderful on these occasions to rejoice in the glory of God's creation as we traversed along the side of St Mary's Loch before returning through beautiful countryside to Peebles. En route we would pass several dams that represent man's impressive engineering ingenuity so enabling the storage of water at high altitude.

Of course a magnificent way to enjoy God's handiwork is to explore on foot. On one of these walks I remember being in the company of Bill Gilvear. Our route took us past the Hartree Hotel, then upwards to the top of the hill before descending into the valley beyond. The notable thing about that valley is that it had been the route adopted by travellers from Edinburgh to Carlisle using horse-drawn carriage.

Bill had come to stay with us for a few days on account of being a bit unwell. I do not suppose we spoke for more than ten minutes during the whole forenoon. My instinct was to leave Bill alone with his own thoughts, just to enjoy the exercise, the view and the serenity of such a place. It was the lambing season and the frolicking of those young creatures in the field just somehow seemed to express the joy of spring and new life. Sometime afterwards, Bill indicated that our silent walk had, he felt, played a significant part in his recovery.

In these days when our role was to provide a service for other people, it was especially helpful to have friends who were a great encouragement to us. Louis and Liz Howson were in that category. They lived in Forth which was about six or eight miles away from Biggar, but still in the countryside. I remember them inviting Nettie and me over for their Sunday morning service. They worshipped in Forth Mission and there were a lot of fine people associated with that fellowship.

An outstanding recollection was that during their communion service, one lady suggested we turn in our Bibles to a passage in I Thessalonians. It was their practice that the person who requested a reading would read the first one or two verses. Then someone else in a very quiet and lovely way would read the next two or three verses and so on until the reading was completed. That impressed me greatly because there was a harmonious progression of male and female voices – something I had never experienced before in a context like that – but it stuck with me and is a memory which I cherish. It reminds me of how much we men are able to benefit from the ministry, broadly speaking, of the ladies and at least one other example is worth mentioning.

The context was being with Alex Lochhead when he was preaching at the Forth Mission Church and I was invited to sing. We had a wonderful tea at the home of Mrs Porteous and her family - the local bakers. Boy, oh boy, did we get a really tremendous spread!! But even the scrumptious meal is not my outstanding memory. That is reserved for going to the prayer meeting prior to the service and hearing women praying for their husbands - some of whom were still battling with alcohol and were apparently far from coming to faith. I remember shedding tears as I listened to these women praying for their husbands. The Biggar experience was certainly a wonderful chapter of our lives.

There came a time when it was obvious to us, however, that we should vacate our personal accommodation in the Centre and find an alternative. It was important to make way for the leadership that followed. One thing that makes me so appreciative of the Lord's hand was the provision of a lovely little flat in the High Street in the town of Biggar. Friends of ours - Joe and Cis Wilson - who were by this time living in Stirling, had always been interested in what we were doing at Maranatha in Biggar and, on many occasions, showed interest in our future, particularly our accommodation needs. These questions were embarrassing because we did not know what to say.

However, it transpired through a conversation Nettie had with Mrs Simpson in the shoe shop, in High Street, Biggar, that she had a flat available that had been recently vacated by her daughter and husband. Nettie was quite excited about this possibility, but I did not show too much interest, knowing that it might be a bit presumptuous of us to think that we could acquire this accommodation.

As time went on, however, that is exactly what happened. Nettie had seen the place and encouraged me to go and have a look. It truly was a lovely little flat. Now here is an interesting fact: the fireplace had been installed by us while we were in the fireplace business!

Joe and Cis called on another occasion and continued to show interest in our future. I ventured to tell them that this little flat had become available. They immediately suggested that they would come over and see it. After a meal with us at Maranatha, we met with the owners. Joe and Cis were so convinced of the rightness of this move for us that they acquired the flat for us and indicated that the house was there for our use for the remainder of the time we would be in Biggar. While we lived there, we continued to work at The Maranatha Conference Centre.

The efficient management of the Centre was crucial to its success and we were blessed with high quality people in that role. We were followed by Kenneth Brown and his wife. Thereafter, Allan and Joan Stevenson took responsibility. They were replaced by Herbie and Jacqui from Ireland and then, subsequently, Alastair and Carol MacKenzie, who had been missionaries for a number of years in Sierra Leone, became our managers. We were also grateful to Willie and Anne Fell, who lived in Douglas, about ten miles away from Biggar. They also did a very good job.

In times when the pressures of life swamp so many, we must not forget the importance of taking time for relaxation and recovery. On one occasion, Jesus advised his disciples, "Come ye apart and rest awhile". Maranatha at Biggar was developed to meet that need and we are grateful for the many hundreds of people who have received its special balm.

At the time of writing these memoirs, the twenty year lease of Maranatha which was given to us in 1986, will imminently expire. We are working very hard even now to find alternative accommodation, and I might say that South Lanarkshire Council, who have no real obligation to us, have been very kind in offering a place so that we may continue the ministry that has gone on for these past number of years at Biggar.

SEVENTEEN: *Mission Scotland '91*

After the incredible success of Dr Billy Graham's preaching in Earls Court in 1954 and in Glasgow in 1955, he returned to the UK on several occasions, for example, to Sheffield in 1985, but my closer involvement with a Billy Graham Crusade was in connection with Mission Scotland '91. I had been associated with landline missions and satellite missions in the interim period. These were means through which modern technology was used to beam the events of a meeting elsewhere in the UK to other venues simultaneously around the country.

Dr Billy Graham preaching at podium

The origin of Mission Scotland '91 was in the context of Billy Graham's visit to the UK in 1989 which was all part of Mission England. It was at that time that Nettie and I were invited by the Billy Graham Evangelistic Association to go to Crystal Palace Sports Stadium in London along with about another eighty people from throughout the UK to meet Mr Graham. My invitation was probably issued on account of my prior involvement in landline and satellite missions.

At the reception – which was followed by a crusade meeting in the stadium - we all had the opportunity, albeit briefly, to meet Mr Graham personally.

When my turn came, I was struggling to know what to say. I remember just asking him if he would consider coming to Scotland. His reply took me by surprise. "My dear brother", he said, "I am just waiting for an invitation". As I left him, I turned to join three young men who were part of the Graham mission team at that time. Two of them later became very firm friends. One was Rick Marshall, who became Mission Director in Glasgow and Edinburgh and Blair Carlsson whom I had known for many years through his coming to Motherwell as a member of the Wheaton Male Chorus. Both these men were held in high esteem by the BGEA.

When I mentioned Mr Graham's response to me, their advice was: "Don't let that comment go! Don't let that slip, because if that's what he said, he really meant it". I took their reaction as being a sincere indication that he *would* come to Scotland if he received an invitation from the right people.

On our return from London to our home in Biggar, I immediately got to work - knowing that any serious invitation would require the involvement of the national church, the Church of Scotland. I knew that at a previous General Assembly, sadly, they had indicated that they would not involve themselves in any mission other than with their own Church of Scotland people. Clearly, this would make issuing an invitation to Billy Graham more difficult. However, I knew one minister who was involved at the Church of Scotland Headquarters at 121 George Street in Edinburgh: Dr Ian Doyle. I knew him from his time of ministering in Motherwell at St Mary's Church. He agreed to meet me and that proved to have a positive outcome.

At an official level, he indicated what I already knew: that the General Assembly had made the decision that there would be no national evangelism with evangelists outside of Scotland. However, the name 'Billy Graham' seemed to work wonders. Dr Doyle along with the Rev Tom Allan and the Rev Peter Bissett had been very much involved in the 'Tell Scotland' movement in the 1950s. This movement had been responsible, in the first place, for the invitation to Billy Graham to preach at Kelvin Hall in 1955.

At the General Assembly in May of the following year, the proposal to invite Billy Graham to Scotland was given 'the nod'. It was not a very enthusiastic 'nod' of acceptance; however, it was a positive move for which I was very glad and thanked God.

Following that, we started to have meetings that brought together key people in the Bible Training Institute - at that time located in Great Western Road in Glasgow - and from those meetings emerged a number of people who were enthusiastic about the proposal. Consequently, three of us were invited to get our heads together to consider who should form the executive committee for the Mission.

The responsibility of the executive was to take full charge of all of the main aspects of organising what was to become a national mission. Along with the Rev Bob McGhee from Falkirk (and a United Free minister whose name I cannot remember but who never showed up following his nomination), we were given the onerous task of helping to set up the executive group.

Our first step was to have an 'away day' at St Ninian's in Crieff, the Church of Scotland Conference Centre. We travelled together, talking all the way, spending a lot of time in prayer, before getting down to constructing an organisational framework within which we put all the names that had been suggested to us, carefully allocating within each area the people we felt might be best suited for the task.

At this time, the work of a BTI staff member, Richard Gibbons, proved to be absolutely indispensable. Richard made contact with thousands of people who had been involved in a variety of ways with satellite and live link activities in relation to evangelism. His purpose was to identify those who could bring their experience to the development of our preparations for a most important mission. In the end, Richard had details of around eleven thousand interested people.

Often, the success of national mission is inseparable from the backing and support given by official bodies and there is none more important, in this context, than the Church of Scotland. To our delight, one outcome of Richard Gibbons's research work was the commitment of no fewer than ten former moderators of the Church of Scotland to Mission Scotland '91.

As we were moving forward, the BGEA representatives were keeping in contact with us and asked for progress meetings on quite a number of occasions. Those who visited most regularly were Walter Smyth, a key person at that time in BGEA, and Blair Carlsson, previously mentioned. It was so interesting to meet with them on the three or four occasions that we convened and, ultimately, it was agreed by BGEA that our invitation would be accepted and that Mr Graham would, indeed, come and preach in Edinburgh, Glasgow and Aberdeen during May and June 1991. The hard work had just begun! We had just over a year to prepare.

It was wonderful to witness the quality people who came together in these early stages of praying and planning. I was thrilled to learn subsequently that two of our prominent churchmen had been keeping in touch with Mr Graham even prior to our initiative and, indeed, they were held in high esteem by BGEA. They were Professor Tom Torrance and Professor Fraser McCluskie - both ex-Moderators of the General Assembly of the Church of Scotland and both known for their evangelical ministry.

In the initial stages, our Chairman was the Rev Frank Gibson (formerly of Motherwell, but, at that time, living and ministering in the Island of Islay). Nevertheless, two other prominent individuals who were very much on my mind were Sir David McNee and George Russell.

Sir David was, at that time, head of the Metropolitan Police. As a young sergeant he had been very much involved in the All Scotland Crusade in 1955. I had watched his progress through the ranks and had prayed for him on many occasions as he moved up through the various major appointments that he held. I felt that he, being such a high profile Christian with very evident organisational skills, would make a good chairman of the executive committee. If I remember correctly, we had to invite him twice before he accepted this major role. He did a wonderful job.

George Russell was well known in evangelical circles in Scotland and a very successful business man. Mission Scotland '91 was going to need a great deal of funding and George Russell was the one person whom I felt had the contacts and business acumen to fulfil the role of "Fundraiser in Chief ". Sadly, in 2004, both George and his wife Moira died - a sad loss to their family, the Christian community and the wider community.

Rick Marshall, a senior staff member of BGEA, became Mission Director. He and his young family moved to Glasgow and were with us for more than a year. He and I spent many nights together visiting areas where someone would have brought church leaders together and our job was to inform and enthuse these leaders and to inspire them to encourage their people to pray and attend the Mission. Rick had been with the Graham organisation for over twenty years and we benefited greatly from his sharp mind and wide experience. Everything he did was bathed in prayer.

The Executive Committee with Dr Billy Graham

I had been invited to take the role of Mission Co-ordinator with the responsibility of establishing a wide range of task groups and setting out their responsibilities. I was very glad to be involved and would happily have done the job on a voluntary basis but was pressed to accept a paid staff position. Just imagine being well paid for a job for which I would have been only too pleased to volunteer.

It was important for the office to be in a central location. Eventually, we decided to rent the entire top floor of the Pentagon Centre, a large building in Washington Street just off the M8 motorway and near to Glasgow city centre.

The office space was very large and required to be subdivided. Most of that was done with movable partitions. However, there was a need for a more permanent structure to the computer room and the mail room. That would require tradesmen coming in to do the job professionally so cue an opportunity to use my local knowledge of likely people capable of doing the job.

Jim Burrows and his wife, Romy, had been good friends of mine for many years. He was the Chief Executive of a company called Fleming Builders just outside Glasgow. I called Jim and within twenty-four hours he came on to the premises, took the necessary measurements and, within a few days, this job was completed. Later when he was asked about the cost of the job I was told that this was his contribution to the Mission and what a contribution that was.

Official Photograph at Parkhead

What a joy it was to see teams of people coming together in a co-ordinated way to reach Scotland for Christ! These teams had to take responsibility for such areas as prayer, counselling and follow up, administration, literature distribution, catering, stadium arrangements, satellite and tele-communication, transport, security, public relations, advertising and publicity, finance.

Typically, a crusade mission with Billy Graham makes a major impact wherever it is held and Scotland in 1991 was no exception. As in 1955, the same gospel was faithfully preached and thousands of enquirers were counselled and followed up. There was massive interest on the part of churches and their members. Even the Mission choir had more than two thousand members!

Nettie: one voice in 2000

As the first meeting in Edinburgh's open-air Murrayfield Stadium was about to get under way, the mass choir began to sing and it was as if its music was lifted to heaven itself. And, of course, heaven alone knows what spiritual impact there was in Scotland at that time as a result of Mission '91.

The co-ordinator at work at Mission Scotland '91

In my co-ordinating role, there were many lessons to be learned, but none more important than the fact that only a small minority of non Christians are likely to attend missions meetings on their own initiative. Research shows that over ninety-four per cent of the people, who respond to Mr Graham's appeal at the close of each service, are people who have been invited and brought along by friends. Thus the success of any mission is greatly impacted by the enthusiasm and efforts of ordinary church members prayerfully inviting friends and neighbours to attend the Mission. Those relationships are also very important in the follow up of those who have been counselled and who have perhaps taken the first tentative step towards faith in the Lord Jesus. _Relationships_ are key to the overall long term success of any mission.

Response to the preaching at Parkhead

If I have one reservation about large missions, it is that, in the area of follow up and discipling, there are often grave weaknesses. There is a wee chorus that I learned many years ago and the words sum up beautifully how I feel about missions and soul winning. It says:

> Lord lay one soul upon my heart,
> And love that soul through me;
> And may I humbly do my part,
> To win that soul for Thee.

Mass evangelism (even now, I am not sure that I like that expression) may sometimes get a bad press and, perhaps even deservedly at times, but if the mass of Christians were to adopt the truth of that 'wee' chorus, things could be so very different.

EIGHTEEN:

More Evangelism on the Home Front

Even such high profile events as Mission '91 are never designed to exist in isolation, instead, they should be important catalysts in the ongoing work of evangelism in the community. So it was that soon after the Billy Graham Mission concluded, we began to think about how we should move on.

Motherwell, September 1992

Sammy Tippet

During Mission Scotland '91, Jessie McFarlane had been the co-chairperson of the Prayer Committee. In that role, she had invited a young American to come to Glasgow to speak on this crucial subject of prayer.

Sammy Tippet, from San Antonio in Texas, had already written several books on prayer. "The Prayer Factor" was one of his earliest and became a best seller. It was translated into a number of languages.

Sammy impressed many people, including me, by his unassuming manner and passion to communicate the great need for prayer in the life of Christians in the life of the church. A powerful preacher of the gospel, Sammy was invited to come for a mission in Motherwell in 1992.

Motherwell welcomes Sammy Tippet

For a period of eight days, Motherwell's Civic Concert Hall was booked and was packed each night as Sammy delivered his message.

During Mission '91, at least five hundred people from the area had joined and participated in the Billy Graham Crusade Choir. More than two hundred of them returned to form the Mission Choir under the leadership of Iain Morris who had been the deputy choir leader at Mission '91. The accompanist in Motherwell was Karen Jack, a music teacher from East Kilbride. The ministry of the choir was greatly appreciated and, by popular request, a video production was prepared and issued by Gospel Video Productions (GVP) from Kilsyth.

At the conclusion of each meeting, Sammy issued an invitation to any who had been stirred by the message to come forward for counselling – and many did just that, every evening. One specific individual circumstance still touches my heart to recall. Among those I had invited to attend was a local hairdresser. Imagine my excitement and delight when, after Sammy preached on the first night, I saw her respond publicly to the invitation. She was counselled on that evening and has gone on very strongly in her Christian faith.

Lanarkshire Christian Union

Ever since my involvement in Mission Scotland '91, I had felt there was a need to continue working with all of the churches in my area. A new opportunity came when, around this time, I was approached by Lanarkshire Christian Union and asked to co-ordinate the activity of this organisation which had a wonderful heart for evangelism but which also needed to be more strongly connected with modern approaches. LCU also seemed a good vehicle to maintain inter-church activity.

Traditionally, LCU arranged 'Tent Evangelical Missions' throughout Lanarkshire and had a great ministry in rural parts of the county using the services of many well known evangelists of their day.

Meanwhile, in 1990, after four happy years spent in Biggar, Nettie and I had moved back to Motherwell because of its closer proximity to the Mission '91 office in Glasgow.

Owing to LCU's history and the fact that it was not tied to any particular denomination, I felt comfortable that I could involve myself with them and re-establish close links in the local community.

And so began my work with LCU. While, traditionally, a variety of missions were arranged in parts of the calendar year, a new concept was introduced and managed from our premises above the Baptist Church in Motherwell. Known as Crossline (Lanarkshire), this was a Christian telephone helpline. It was first brought to my attention by Alex Lochhead who had picked up a leaflet advertising Crossline (Edinburgh) and, as was his habit, passed it on to me to activate in Lanarkshire. I thought it was a good idea and proceeded to implement it by contacting a number of people that I considered might be interested in being part of the team. From 10am to 10pm, this dedicated group of trained counsellors sensitively responded to the various callers. As circumstances allowed, sometimes the caller would be invited to our headquarters where private areas were provided for further confidential discussion and counselling. We have so many reasons to be grateful for the sustained dedication of counsellors that included John and Jessie Hewitt, Louise Robertson, Alison McCracken, Donald Plant, Sandy Steen and others.

Power to Live

It was our intention to encourage and inspire evangelism throughout the area and one of the early opportunities arose in connection with the Monklands district of Lanarkshire.

Two young Church of Scotland probationers had expressed to me a desire to reach the young people of the Monklands area of Lanarkshire (Airdrie, Coatbridge, Plains, Caldercruix). These ministers were Rev Jim Stewart (who now ministers in an exciting Church of Scotland charge in Perth) and the Rev Jim Ritchie (whose ministry has now taken him to Aberdeen).

As a result of their enthusiasm and the important fact that they were Church of Scotland ministers, they were able to bring many churches together to support them in their proposed outreach in Monklands.

Because of my trust in these young men and my involvement with LCU, we were able to get behind their vision and kick-start the Mission with a gift of fifteen hundred pounds. As an older person attending the prayer meetings, it was tremendously uplifting for me to experience the fervour and excitement of these young people - and this did my heart a lot of good.

The build up to the Mission was well planned. The prayer convenors were two young ladies whose enthusiasm and evident spirituality were infectious. Others who were involved with the 'two Jims' set the tone for a very successful mission. They visited all the secondary schools in the area and gained fairly unrestrained access to eight secondary schools, including two Catholic schools.

The evangelist who was invited to speak to the young people in the evenings was John McKinnon who had, for a number of years, been with Scripture Union. His ability to communicate with young people in Scotland was first class.

The programme for the Mission meetings incorporated a variety of bands and Christian entertainers such as Rod and Marco. These guests were also able to visit schools during the day and to conclude their time there with an invitation for young people to make their way to Airdrie Town Hall where they could experience the official programme.

Each evening, between three and four hundred young people turned up for the meeting. I visited the venue on a few occasions and, sitting in the balcony, I could observe all that was going on. The volume of the bands brought havoc to my hearing but the young people were excited by the programme. They applauded everything they heard and were very vocal in their appreciation. During the preliminary part of the programme, they even moved about quite freely.

However, what amazed me was that when John McKinnon stood up to speak, they were completely silent. At the end of each evening, an invitation was given to come forward to know more about the Christian faith. A total of one hundred and eighty-seven young people had conversation at that point with trained counsellors and were given literature to help them to come to faith, if they had not already done so. I was thrilled with the thoroughness and commitment of those involved and have prayed often that such a mission would be replicated in other parts of Lanarkshire.

One other thing that caused me to rejoice was that, a year or so after Mission Monklands, I had a telephone call from the headmaster of a Catholic school in Bellshill. He was a former head of a school in Monklands and asked that he be kept informed if we were considering doing something similar in his area. I continue to pray that this may happen.

A fire was lit in Monklands at that time and I pray that the flame will never be extinguished. Many people from various parts of Central Scotland inquired about the Mission and how it had come about. I pray that it will be a helpful model for things to come.

The question might be asked as to whether evangelistic missions still have a place in the twenty-first century. Our natural inclination in these days of media awareness and the world of the soundbyte is to assume that we have to be 'clever' in our approach. Certainly, we need to be relevant but scripture makes it clear that it is by the so-called "foolishness of preaching" that many are saved and, in whatever context it is delivered, the preaching of God's Word will always have my full support.

And so to the future. As I look ahead, honesty calls on me to express concern about Christian witness in our area and in our land. So many congregations and Christian groups are struggling and looking at a very bleak future. Diminishing congregations in the Church of Scotland are merging with one another and the challenges of growth seem to represent an impossible task. The sadness is that so many in leadership seem content just to maintain the status quo - this notwithstanding the fact that *some* churches *are* developing and growing.

One perception that makes me particularly sad is that I see groups of churches and congregations that place themselves under the banner "evangelical" but they do not *engage* in evangelism. Successful evangelism cannot be divorced from evangelical activity; there must be a *mobilisation* of the membership of our churches. Some of the evidence for that lies in the success of such initiatives as "Alpha" and "Christianity Explored". But ministers, pastors and elders cannot complete the task alone. Ephesians 4, verse 12, instructs leaders "to prepare God's people for works of service so that the body of Christ may be built up". My conviction is this is not happening enough. In other parts of the world, notably Africa, South America and parts of Asia, we hear of revivals and times of great blessing where countless numbers are turning to God through faith in Jesus Christ. I find it significant that the main social difference between many of these areas of the world and the western world which *we* inhabit is represented by the word 'affluence'. I believe materialism is at the root of our apathy and affects our passion for the "lost" and drives underground our enthusiasm for evangelism.

Verse 11 of Ephesians 4 lists the gifts that God has given His people. Gifts are given to each one of us and we need to use them in the process of reaching out to friends, associates and families.

NINETEEN : *Teamwork for the Kingdom*

Throughout most of my life I have seen the value of teamwork, especially when it involves Christians working together for the greater goal: the glory of God and the extension of His kingdom.

In setting up the Maranatha Centre, we never proposed that it become yet another parachurch organisation with separate identity and disconnected from the broader areas of Christian work in the vicinity. By contrast, I believe it is absolutely essential that 'working together' as a whole church community is of immense importance and I have been privileged over many years to be instrumental in helping put a jigsaw piece or two in place to extend the bigger picture of Christian witness in the area.

The Establishment of the GLO Centre in Motherwell

On one occasion, the Maranatha Junior Singers had been invited to take part in an annual social evening arranged for Sunday School Superintendents, teachers and Bible Class leaders from various Churches of Scotland in our area. I was there to introduce the choir and to make linking comments, as and when required.

During a break for tea, I was congratulating Rev William Bruce of Dalziel Parish Church about how good the sanctuary looked after its recent re-decoration. It is a beautiful building that holds around twelve hundred people. Clearly delighted by my comments, Rev Bruce replied that, if I ever required a venue for the choir or any other Christian purpose, he would be delighted to make the building available to us at no charge. This impressed me greatly, particularly the 'no charge' part.

During the evening, I did mention how much the choir was enjoying the space available on the stage of the main hall and contrasted this with how cramped we were for space at Maranatha, where the junior singers and the senior choir both met on a Friday night. It was really quite difficult to accommodate everybody.

At the end of that evening, Mr Bruce returned to the subject of assisting us and suggested that he would like to set up a meeting involving their Session Clerk.

Dalziel Parish Church sat side by side with the Marshall Church, thereby forming a vast complex which I used to call the Holy Island. The second of these churches was becoming available as congregations merged. Suddenly, there was an incredible offer: would I be interested in discussing the possibility of acquiring the Marshall complex for the Maranatha Centre? I was astonished at such a proposal and indicated that I was most grateful.

A meeting was arranged in order that I meet the elders of Dalziel Parish Church which, by then, had united with the Marshall Church. Having been brought up in Ebenezer Gospel Hall, I thought that 'meeting the elders' would maybe mean about eight to twelve people convening, at the most.

I remember returning from Carstairs Hospital (where, as Maranatha, we conducted Bible studies and various other activities) to attend the meeting at Dalziel Parish. I was accompanied by my friend, Jack Watt, who was the treasurer at Maranatha.

On arriving at the church, I was taken to meet the Kirk Session and was dumbfounded to discover that this body comprised some eighty-six people including elders, deacons and other leaders in the church. I was put into the hot seat to be asked questions. I felt totally out of my depth, but because of the prayer requests leading up to this meeting, I felt a bit more at ease and strengthened as I answered the questions.

Eventually, there came the query about how much we would be prepared to pay for the building! I indicated to these good folks that this would be where our conversation would likely end because we did not have any funds and would not voluntarily involve ourselves in debt. However, I do remember saying: "Friends, I feel that if this building goes to any other group of people other than a Christian Ministry, it would be a very sad day". I did not know at that time that the Freemasons were interested in the building and that the Council had also shown an interest in the complex becoming a heritage centre.

However, within a month or two, the building was offered to me at the ludicrously low rent of five pounds per year. This was an amazing circumstance, but even during the time I had been involved in these discussions, I knew that this place was much too big to be effectively used by the Maranatha Centre and it was to transpire that the Lord had different plans.

Around that time, it had come to my notice that the folks in Gospel Literature Outreach were looking for premises in Motherwell. I had the privilege and pleasure of meeting with them. I especially remember Colin Tilsley (who died not many years later), the man used by God to set up Gospel Literature

Outreach – a Christian ministry with a locus in several parts of the world. GLO wanted to establish their European headquarters in Motherwell.

Again, I met the leaders of Dalziel Parish Church, and it was mutually agreed that the building would be passed over to GLO and I thank God for that. The work has grown immensely and not only houses a fine coffee shop and Christian book store, but is a Bible training centre that attracts students from the UK and beyond. Many of them go on to serve full time in Christian ministry in the UK or overseas.

Hamilton College

One Wednesday, in May 1982, on the early evening news there was an item about Hamilton College – a building which had lain empty for a number of years. The point of the news item was that a Christian group from England had expressed an interest in acquiring the building in order to establish a Christian school. Apart from wondering what kind of group this might be, I did not think about the matter too much during the rest of the evening, which was largely spent at our weekly prayer meeting.

Later that evening, on my return, Nettie told me that a man from the Liverpool area would be telephoning. The caller was Charles Oxley. I had never heard of him but it was he who was behind the bid for Hamilton College. On the previous evening, Mr Oxley had been interviewed in Preston by Norman Lochhead, son of Alex Lochhead.

On recognising Norman's Scottish accent, Mr Oxley announced that he was interested in buying a property in Hamilton and enquired as to whether Norman knew anyone in the area who might be able to help. My telephone number was passed to him.

Incidentally, Norman had been recording an interview for "Red Rose Radio", one of the early independent radio stations. It was a great joy for me to know Norman had his early training when he was a member of the Maranatha Centre's recording team.

The purpose of Mr Oxley's telephone call to me was to ask if I would meet with him. Our rendezvous took place in the tearoom in the main building of Strathclyde Country Park. It seemed strange to me at the time that we drank tea from plastic cups, but at least this venue afforded us a view across the River Clyde towards the college building. Before we finished talking, we both prayed for the success of the proposed school project. I took the responsibility of bringing together key people who could give Mr Oxley local advice about the Scottish Educational system. Among them were Harry Morris (a Senior Schools' Inspector) and Iain Morris (Head of English at Airdrie Academy). I also put Mr Oxley in touch with Robert MacGillivray (Accountant), Alan MacGregor the Manager of the Bank of Scotland in Motherwell, John Hunter (Lawyer) and others. These meetings were held in the Garrion Hotel in Motherwell - now the Headquarters of Social Services in North Lanarkshire. Mr Oxley appreciated greatly the help and guidance received from these professional people.

In May 1982, the bid of two hundred and seventy thousand pounds was accepted by the Council. That, in turn, caused a furore. When the college was built, it cost two million pounds and it is on record that it would cost around twenty million pounds to build it today. There were some, in the local area, deeply opposed to the sale at such a price. On the other hand, considering how long the building had lain empty and how the market works, one could easily argue that the sum paid by Mr Oxley's organisation was a great deal better than what anyone else was prepared to pay.

I have followed the progress of the school over the years and I am always thrilled to visit from time to time and to witness the demeanour and good behaviour of the young people, as always, rigged out in their distinctive school uniform.

The teachers and governors at the college continue to be of a very high calibre and I am favoured to meet with them each year as an invited lunch guest prior to the annual prize giving and speech day service.

It is always good to read in the local press of the academic achievements of the college. It is worthy of note, too, that at least twenty per cent of the students at the college are of Asian origin, many of them from Muslim and non-faith backgrounds. The attraction for the parents, of course, is the high academic attainment of the school's pupils and the discipline arising from its strong Christian ethos.

In a society in which Christianity appears increasingly under pressure, both morally and statistically, every opportunity needs to be taken to heighten its profile and influence. I feel privileged to have played even a small part in the process.

TWENTY : *New Life for Mananatha*

During my time of working with Lanarkshire Christian Union, I became acutely aware that the Maranatha Centre in Glencairn Street had been closed and there was a possibility of the building being put up for sale.

You will recall that, having moved to Biggar, I had retired from work at the Maranatha Centre in Motherwell. On my return, I learned that those in charge had been suffering serious financial challenges and, indeed, had decided that the building should be sold. However, they were still hopeful that some positive solution could be found. I had expressed my concern and was invited to meet with the people who had been brought in to see if we could find a way to keep the centre going. I have always been convinced that the Maranatha Centre had been provided by God for the care and benefit of young people in the area and I had no clear conviction that the Centre did not any more have a future in that regard. Those responsible for the management of the Centre had, in the interim, felt led to develop the emphasis from outreach to a concern with people who were socially deprived and those with alcohol and drug related problems.

During this time of financial crisis, I visited the Centre on a number of occasions and was greatly impressed by the work being done with those unfortunate people. The main area downstairs had been altered to become a very attractive tearoom and restaurant with a fully equipped modern kitchen. After a few years, it was not possible to pay the bills and, at the time of my being invited to discuss the situation, there was a substantial financial crisis.

The outcome of our conversations was that I accepted the responsibility of a new challenge facing the Maranatha Centre: to review its purpose, to suggest a way ahead and to bring back financial stability.

I remember very well the day I took the keys, conscious of the fact that the mantle was resting on me, aged seventy-five. (At time of writing, I am now eighty-one going on a hundred!) Yet, I have so much to thank God for in giving me the opportunity of, again, proving His faithfulness, His guidance and His protection.

On taking up responsibility once again at the Maranatha Centre, I transferred the work of Lanarkshire Christian Union from Motherwell Baptist Church - where it had been located for around five years - to the Maranatha Centre.

As I look back on my involvement with LCU, I do so with gratitude as it had brought me into contact with godly men and women who had served their Lord over many years but I felt that LCU had perhaps achieved what God had intended of it and my interest re-focused now on a vision shared many years earlier with my dear friends Alex Lochhead, Sam Hill, Billy Gilmour, Robert Forrest and Bert Young.

When Nettie and I returned from Biggar, in a sense, we were 'of no fixed abode'! We had temporary accommodation in the manse of the Baptist Church before moving to a small flat in Freesia Court. This, we thought would be our last house move. One day, however, a visit from a very good friend of mine, Douglas Park, changed all that. As a consequence, Nettie and I, in a circumstance beyond our wildest dreams, found ourselves moving into the penthouse at Park Court in Auchingramont Road in Hamilton. For this privilege, I will never cease to be grateful. We were well and truly back in the area.

Meanwhile, the challenge at Maranatha was that we had a building but no ministry. This situation cast me on the Lord in real earnest prayer. I do think it takes a situation like this for us to get "real" in our prayers. So often we say prayers with little conviction and lack the expectation of our prayers being answered. I think those reading this will understand what I am saying: that if we have no vision, no burning desire to see God work in our lives, we get to 'saying' prayers without necessarily 'praying'. I know – I've been there and it is not the best place to be. As we read in Proverbs: "Where there is no vision, the people perish".

But vision needs to *come* from somewhere. In 2001, I was invited by the Herald's Trust to a conference in Gartmore House in the famously beautiful Trossachs district of Scotland. The subject to be addressed was "Effective Leadership in a Rapidly Changing World". The main speaker was Dr Joseph Stowell, at that time, the principal of the Moody Bible Institute in Chicago, USA. This was a very worthwhile encounter.

Nettie was unwell at this time and so I was very reluctant to leave her. Consequently, I spent only two days and one overnight at Gartmore. Nevertheless, a very wonderful thing happened there. After the first plenary session, we were each allocated to be part of a group that would discuss what had been said by the speaker. The person chairing my group was David Clarkston from Cartsbridge Evangelical Church in Glasgow. In time-honoured fashion, he suggested that each group member introduce themselves and include mention of the involvement each of us had in Christian service.

A gentleman in the corner of the room said: "My name is Norman Lynas. I come from Port Stewart in Northern Ireland and I am working with young people." He went on to give a brief description of his ministry, part of which included the "Exodus" project. I don't remember anything else that took place during that session because I could not escape quickly enough to speak to this man.

In earlier years, I had taken young people from my Bible Class and the Maranatha Centre to Port Stewart to join with other young people from the province in an Ulster/Scottish Crusade based at the town hall and led by the evangelist Hedley Murphy. Knowing Port Stewart as a small holiday town, I found it difficult to imagine important work with young people going on there.

Norman reached into his pocket and gave me a rather tatty little brochure. After reading it and listening to him describe how God was blessing this work, I knew why the Lord had directed me to be at Gartmore that day and realised what He was doing in Port Stewart, He could do in Motherwell. I wanted to know more.

I needed to follow up with a visit and the opportunity to do so presented itself.

Each July, Nettie and I were invited by our good friends Walter and Sharon Watson to spend two weeks with them at their lovely home in Castlewellan in the beautiful mountains of Mourne in County Down. On our next visit, I was able to travel north to Port Stewart, courtesy of the Watson's youngest boy Graeme (who, along with his wife, is working full time in Christian ministry in the USA). I was able to visit the "Exodus" project in Port Stewart and be shown around by one of the trustees. Thereafter, Norman Lynas and his colleague Jim Brown visited us in Motherwell and I have been able to make further visits to Port Stewart and also to their new venue at Coleraine.

I became convinced that what they were doing, we needed to emulate. Now we had premises and a vision for what we wanted to do but no staff to carry out the work to help fulfil the vision.

It had perplexed me, however, that Norman Lynas, chairman of "Exodus", had counselled me in the following way: "Wallace, don't advertise for a full time worker. **Pray** and allow God to lead you to the right people." He added that I should share the vision and the need only with a few friends in leadership in our local area. Waiting is not my strongest attribute, but wait I did.

Waiting was, indeed, to become an important part of my experience at this time. Nettie was getting quite ill, with doctors and consultants seemingly unable to get to the root of her health problems. One day around then I had a call from Eleanor Simpson, whose husband Bill I had confided in. Eleanor told me that on the previous evening, some minister friends had visited their home and had been discussing the work and needs of the Maranatha Centre. During their conversation, they indicated that they knew a young man who had been involved in a successful business but was selling up and would like to work full time with young people. The problem was that Eleanor did not have his name or telephone number but promised to call me back with the information. It might have been providence that led to delay in that information coming because other personal matters were about to occupy my full attention.

Eventually, Nettie's illness was diagnosed as cancer and everything else was set to one side in the hope that, with modern treatment and medication, she would get well. Nettie was not only my wife and the mother of our three children, but my partner in every venture. She was the centre of my life and I leant on her more than anyone would ever know. For example, when we finished in business, she was the one who was the stronger. Never once did she show anger or annoyance at what had taken place - particularly when we had to sell our house and cars and be obliged to friends to give us a roof over our heads. She accepted all of that without any rancour whatsoever. We had courted for four and a half years and been married for fifty five and a half years – in all, sixty wonderful years.

Our Golden Wedding

Nettie died on 7 March, 2002 and there were many wonderful tributes to her. I miss her a whole lot.

It was about a month after Nettie's death that Eleanor Simpson called me. She had delayed passing on the information, knowing the upset we had experienced. Now she had that key fact for me.

The young man in question was Neil MacLennan. I called him at his home in Glasgow and within forty-eight hours he visited me at my home in Hamilton. It is difficult to put into words the excitement I felt as I experienced God answering my prayers. A young man of thirty years of age, he had been very successful in business and his one desire now was to work full time with young people. After sharing all that was on my mind with regard to re-opening Maranatha, we went to Motherwell so that he could see the building for himself and both of us continued to share what was in our hearts. We parted with Neil promising that he would call me as to whether he felt he was ready to make the commitment. This he did within twenty-four hours.

An interview took place within a week. I attended with three others, who were also very much interested in the work at Maranatha – Liz McCully, William Kirkland (no relation) and my son Archie.

During that week, there was a lot of prayer as I prepared. During the run up to the interview, I noted twenty questions that I would like to have Neil answer. The moment arrived and, after introducing Neil to the others and committing our time together to the Lord, we experienced such a unity of spirit.

First, Neil was asked to tell us about his life and journey of faith. By the time he had concluded his comments, which were very comprehensive, there was no need for me to ask any further question. All had been covered in his earlier response. The meeting was concluded and Neil left. As we pondered over the time spent with him, there was unanimous agreement that he was the person that God was bringing among us. We concluded with a prayer of grateful thanks to the One who was, indeed, answering our prayers.

Once Neil had finalised his own business commitments, he commenced full time in August 2002 as Manager of the Maranatha Centre.

During this time, another young man had been brought to our notice by Pastor Hugh Clark of the Kings Church in Motherwell. Hugh was one of the six leaders I had previously contacted. The young man in question was Colin McIlvenna. Colin had enrolled for training at the International Christian College in Glasgow for a three year course. There was a scheme in operation at the college whereby students were given placements for practical involvement. The Maranatha Centre was the kind of place that would offer him just such an opportunity.

Through Neil's leadership, the work in Maranatha Centre has been firmly re-focused on the spiritual needs of young people and, while there have been difficulties and challenges, we are grateful that, coinciding with the publication of this book, we are able to celebrate the fiftieth anniversary of the work established those many years ago in an old knitwear factory.

In the meantime, while retaining a position on our executive committee, Neil has re-positioned his ministry within a Church of Scotland in Bo'ness and we are grateful that the mantle of responsibility is with Colin McIlvenna as Maranatha moves past its half century and steps into the future.

TWENTY-ONE : *Family Matters*

As I reflect on so many jigsaw pieces that have combined to make the life of Wallace Kirkland, I can say with absolute conviction that the most meaningful aspect of life is not so much the things that happened, but the people with whom I formed relationships. Among the closest relationships one can experience on earth are with one's family and that is the subject of this chapter.

Ultimately, of course, the most important and significant relationship is with God. Without that spiritual connection to eternity, our lives surely will end in disaster. It is through our connection with Jesus Christ that we are able to step from time into a blessed eternity that we can enjoy forever in His presence.

Photograph by Sharp of Hamilton

The relationships that we enjoy on earth are, in many respects, an echo of the relationships we enjoy with God. Scripture pictures the relationship between Christ and His church as the preparation for marriage. Christ is the Bridegroom; the church is His Bride. No-one can have read the preceding pages of this book without recognising how much my relationship with my wife, Nettie, meant to me and one of its tremendously enhancing features is that, together, we have been responsible, in human terms, for the creation of new life and knew the joy and privilege of bringing family into the world. In turn, our children have provided us with grandchildren and the generation after that has also begun.

At this moment, I am father to three children, grandfather to seven and great-grandfather to one. Compared to father Abraham, these 'achievements' may seem insignificant, but each one of them is of special importance in my life and, of course, as our children have grown up and married, the family has been enlarged by other wonderful 'children-in-law' that we have joyfully 'adopted' into the family: Barbara's husband, Alan Law; Archie's wife, Joyce and Jimmy's wife, Margaret. Without doubt, family life is a blessing that comes from God.

There is a wonderful balance - one might even say 'symmetry' - about family relationships. When children are born into the world, they are in a state of helplessness and are utterly dependent on their parents for their very survival. Over the first two decades of life, there is increasing independence and then, for most young people, there is almost complete independence - by which time, the parents who so faithfully sustained their children in their early years are becoming more dependent on the very children to whom they first gave life.

Allan and Joan Stevenson

Nettie and I were privileged not only to bring up children but, in our later years, to benefit from their love and care. That means so much to me. I am blessed in so many ways: Barbara visits me four to five times a year; my daughters-in-law, Margaret and Joyce, look after me so very well. The care I receive on a regular basis extends beyond the family. Jessie Donald will phone me at least once a week to tell me she has left soup at the door. Ken and Vi Philip are also very caring in how they look after me - and the property. And I never forget how now for ten and a half years I have lived in a beautiful apartment home through the kindness of Douglas Park. I thank God for all of these good people every day.

One is aware of other families where there is division and separation and all kinds of dissent. Perhaps, as they look back, their recollections are often filled with offence and hurt. It is so important that such matters are set to one side and that reconciliation and forgiveness are allowed to bring healing and a restoration of relationship.

I thank God for relationship and the strength and warmth of a loving family, not least of all because it brings balance and order to life. Sometimes, of course, that sense of order and balance may be disrupted by what, from a human point of view, appears to be calamity.

Alan and Barbara

My daughter, Barbara, married Alan Law in October 1972. Their relatively young lives were to be disrupted in 1996 by Alan's seemingly untimely death from cancer when he was aged only forty-seven. For much of his early life, Alan Law lived on 'the wild side'. In his teens, he ran away from home and, similar to so many young people, tried to find fulfilment in what he would have called 'freedom'. But such 'freedom', so-called, is merely another name for bondage to one's own desires. With absolute certainty, and on the authority of scripture, we can say that only if "the Son will set you free, you will be free indeed".

Vividly, I remember Alan Law having returned, with a great sense of prodigality, coming to chat with me in the Maranatha Centre. Without reserve, he poured out his heart about his goings on in 'the far country'. I listened to what he told me with a mixture of dismay and sadness because my own tender conscience reminded me about the similarity between what I was hearing and how I had lived in earlier years. It was as if part of my past was revisiting me.   But the wonderful evidence before me was that here was a boy who wanted, at last, to find stability in his life in a relationship with Jesus Christ. Gladly, I was able to confirm to him that our God is always longing to forgive those who come to Him in repentance and faith.

Shortly afterwards, I discovered that Barbara and Alan had shown a mutual interest in each other and were going out together. I confess that, after hearing some of the stories which Alan had related to me in confidence, my heart did not leap with joy. Soon it became obvious that this relationship was going to last and Barbara and Alan announced their intention to get married. Even then, I regret to say, I had more concern than joy about the future of this relationship, but God had a plan for Alan's life which became a great rebuke to me in my misgivings.

Alan Law

Alan Law was deeply serious about giving his life to God. He registered at the Bible Training Institute in Glasgow, the predecessor of today's International

Christian College. Not having had, shall we say, a deeply fruitful educational experience in his earlier years, academic study was to prove a major challenge to him. Yet it was with great pride that, one day, he received a special accolade at an award ceremony for being the student who had made the greatest progress. Afterwards, I used to joke with him that, given his lowly starting point, progress was inevitable!

By God's strength and help, Alan graduated from BTI and made himself available to go into full time ministry and, miraculously, God opened up the way. One could have supposed that Alan's pastoral future might have lain in working with young tearaways somewhere in the heart of Glasgow - but not so! He was called to a church in Cambridge - a symbol of upper class prestige and academia.

But a young man brought up in the environs of Glasgow and used to speaking at a hundred miles an hour with a Scottish accent for sure experienced some communication challenges in the heart of Cambridgeshire! But it was nothing that tuition in elocution could not fix and, once again, I smiled wryly in seeing how this son-in-law of mine was revisiting some of my own experiences of earlier life.

Alan became Associate Pastor in Great Shelfort Baptist Church. There, the young tearaway from Coatbridge was able to minister to people who were academically out of his league and yet here was more evidence of how God's spirit can produce the impossible from lives that are dedicated to Him. Life was good for Alan and Barbara and God had blessed them with three children: Andrew, Ruth and David.

So it was with a great sense of mystery and concern that we learned some years later that Alan was afflicted by cancer. In the latter stages of his illness and clearly knowing that death was virtually certain, he was removed from the hospice in which he had received tender care and taken back home to spend his final days. Well I remember Sunday 19 May 1996 - the day on which he went into the Lord's presence. Around his earthly remains stood his mum, his five sisters and his only brother. Nettie and I, along with Barbara and the three children, were also present. At the moment he died, there was what I can only describe as an explosion of grief, but it was followed by an unbelievable spiritual calm as we simply placed our future into the hands of the Lord. One memory deeply imprinted on my recollection is that of Alan's youngest son, David, lying beside his recently departed father's body with his head tucked under his father's arm.

Memorial to Alan Law

If I say that the funeral a few days later was an occasion to be spiritually savoured, I am sure you will not misunderstand my sentiments. The church was filled to overflowing and, unusually, the decision was taken that those attending the funeral would walk the distance of almost two miles from the church to the graveyard. What an astonishing testimony in the area. Nobody had seen anything quite like it. Death will not have the final say for those who belong to Christ. "Oh death, where is your sting? Oh grave, where is your victory?" Christian experience teaches us that God can and does bring forth a shout of victory from even the darkest experiences on earth. But even that is no more than a foretaste of the ultimate victory which we will experience when, on a future day, God will bring *all things* together under Christ as head. His total victory is absolutely assured.

> *Thine be the glory, risen, conquering Son,*
> *Endless is the victory, thou o'er death hast won.*

The word 'endless' inspires me for it leaves absolutely no room for defeat - ever.

I have chosen, in this chapter, to concentrate on the dramatic experience of Alan and Barbara but that is not in any way intended to eclipse my love and concern for every member of my family for every one has their own special place in my heart and I name them lovingly before God every day.

Daughter Barbara and her family...
Ruth and her husband Michael and my great grandson, Archie
Andrew and his wife Beca
David

Son Archie and his wife Joyce and their children...
Cheryl and Scott

Son Jimmy and his wife Margaret and their children...
Mark and Richard

In 1971, my album "The Happy Heart" was produced and is included with this book. Truly, what will make my earthly happiness complete is to know that every one of these dear children has a personal faith in Jesus Christ that will allow us all to spend eternity together.

TWENTY-TWO : *Lasting Thoughts*

As, in my eighties, I look back over my life, I do so with the most sincere thankfulness to God for preserving me through all of those years. Mine has been an eventful life. Major lessons have been learned - sometimes through bitter experience and as a consequence of my own self-will and sinfulness, but also, too, lessons are learned as we come to accept that God's way is best. As I often recall: "Each victory will help you some other to win."

I truly believe that for each person - including the wayward one - who has truly come to faith in the Lord Jesus Christ there is a God ordained plan. If we are genuinely humbled and devoted to the Lord in *every* area of our life, great things can be achieved. Truly, it has been said that the world has yet to see what can be achieved or accomplished by one who is *totally committed* to following the Lord. Therein lies the challenge. Too often, those who have been greatly gifted and with so much potential for good, fail because of some flaw in their personality that has not been placed on the altar.

When I look at my life, there is so much for which I am grateful, but, most of all, it is the grace of God, for I can say with assurance, that compared to His standard: "In me there dwelleth no good thing". Looking back, I am thrilled, nevertheless, that He has chosen me to be part of His great plan and that, in so many ways throughout eight decades, I can see His hand upon my life. It is also well summarised in a hymn which I love to sing:

> *I am amazed that God could ever love me*
> *So full of sin, so covered over with shame*
> *Make me to walk with Him who is above me*
> *Cleansed by the power of His redeeming grace*
>
> *I am amazed that God would deign to bless me*
> *Chose me, an heir, to riches of His grace*
> *'Till that perfection doth at last possess me*
> *He has reserved for all who seek His face*

> **Chorus**
> *I am amazed that God would ever love me*
> *Naught but His cross could take away my sin*
> *Through faith in Christ eternal life He gave me*
> *Now He abides forever more within.*

Singing has always been a big part of my life and so many of the hymns I have chosen to sing had to affect my life before I could minister them to anyone else. And they did affect me in a very big way.

On one occasion, I had been singing at a Gideon conference at Crieff Hydro and among those attending was Mr Williamson, Chief Constable of Northampton. About a week or so after this event, Mr Williamson telephoned to ask if I would record a hymn – "Saved By Grace" - and send the recording to him. Well, at that time, I had never even heard of the song and if you knew the difficulty I have in learning new songs... If I heard someone sing something that I really liked, then I would have no problem in picking it up, but learning a new song that I had never heard anyone else sing posed a great difficulty. I have no technical skill in reading music whatsoever. For me to learn something new, Nettie had to play the music a number of times, record it and then I had to work on the words with the recorded music.

In the case of "Saved By Grace", the words so gripped me as I struggled to learn them that, when given the opportunity to record the album known as "The Happy Heart", I chose the hymn, "Saved By Grace" as the first hymn on the record.

As you read the hymn at the end of this chapter, I hope, like me, you will be greatly challenged by the brevity of time and by the fact that, one day sooner than we can imagine, those of us who are "saved by grace" will be face to face with the Lord - and what a wonderful day that will be. I am sure that the writer of the hymn was inspired by the words of Ephesians 2 verses 8, 9: "It is by grace you have been saved through faith and this not from yourselves; it is the gift of God; not of works so that no-one can boast." A powerful message to us all.

I have often been inspired by the hymn writing of the blind poetess, Fanny Crosbie. One day I came across the following point of information about her. A minsiter had remarked to her one day on how sad it was that she had lost her sight. She replied that it was not such a problem, adding that one blessing of which she was sure was "that when the Lord calls me home, His shall be the first face I will ever see."

I trust as you have read this record of my life, you will see why I chose to begin these memoirs with praise on my lips: surely goodness and mercy **have** followed me all the days of my life. The words that follow form a crucial bridge to dwelling "in the house of the Lord for ever".

Some day the silver cord will break
And I no more, as now, shall sing
But oh what joy when I awake
Within the palace of my King

Chorus
And I shall see Him face to face
And tell the story saved by grace
And I shall see Him face to face
And tell the story saved by grace

Some day my earthly house will fall
I cannot tell how soon twill be
But this I know my all in all
Has now a place in Heaven for me

Some day 'till then I'll watch and wait
My lamp all trimmed and burning bright
That when my Saviour opens the gate
My soul to Him may take its flight

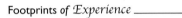

Epilogue

For much of my life, I have tried to fan the flame of enthusiasm for evangelism in my own life and in the lives of others. The writing of this book in my eighties may be one of the last significant activities in which I engage. If, in doing so, I am able to contribute even in a small way either to kindling or fuelling your passion for evangelism, then I will consider the effort worthwhile. May God bless each and every one of you as you play your part in spreading the gospel in our land and in our world.

Yours, in Christian love,

Wallace